GW01086965

Stem Cell Research and Cloning: Contemporary Challenges to Our Humanity

edited by

D Gareth Jones

and

Mary Byrne

ATF Press
Adelaide

Interface 7/2 (October 2004)

Stem Cell Research and Cloning: Contemporary Challenges to Our Humanity

Contents

Interface 7/2 (October 2004)

Stem Cell Research and Cloning: Contemporary Challenges to Our Humanity

Editorial

In August this year the government in Britain approved the granting of licences to research groups who wished to research and develop the cloning of human embryos for therapeutic purposes. The main focus of such research is the attainment of embryonic stem cells, and the development of therapies from such cells. Already some of this research is reported to be happening in South Korea. While they were initially discussed as separate issues in ethical and theological debates, they are now closely intertwined. The first group in England to receive a licence predicts that they will be successful within the next few years. This adds an intensity to our need to understand the dimensions of this science and its impact on our life as well as our desire to put a meaning to these developments. In this edition of *Interface* five authors have offered their contributions to the conversation discussing both cloning and stem cells and how these continue to challenge contemporary notions of our humanity.

The contributions of Jones and Finlay are both predicated on the assumption that discussions of this ilk should be informed by accurate science. This is not to say that the discussions are to be solely guided by the agendas of the scientific community, but that theological and ethical debate that lacks a firm anchorage in the minutiae of scientific debate may be less than helpful. After all, discussions about stem cells and cloning are discussions about scientific ventures, whatever other implications they may have for humanity. They would not be taking place were it not for the activities of scientists in scientific laboratories. Consequently, the issues that arise are ones that originate from outside the traditional domains of theology, although they may be seen as central to some branches of applied theology.

Even the conclusion that such work should not be taking place entails a precise knowledge of the scope of the work and its probable repercussions. To attempt to prohibit a whole area of scientific endeavour on the grounds that it will lead to X and Y, when that is not the case, is at best seriously misleading. This comes to the fore in the debate over the respective scientific value of embryonic as opposed to adult stem cells. While it is perfectly legitimate to argue against the use of embryonic stem cells on theological or moral grounds (regardless of their respective scientific value), a boundary is crossed once this moral or theological argument looks to scientific data for support. To argue for the moral superiority of adult stem cells over their embryonic counterparts, on the ground that they are of greater scientific or clinical utility, is to conflate two distinct approaches. In addition, if such an argument is to be valid a detailed knowledge of the scientific issues and of their ever-changing complexions is essential.

Even when it is argued that the crux of the matter is the status of the human embryo, and that this has nothing to do with scientific perspectives, the latter are invariably invoked to bolster a position reached on theological, moral or social grounds. Genetic and embryological concepts are repeatedly utilised in this manner, even though they generally occupy a subsidiary role. Nevertheless, any use of such concepts requires that they be accurately interpreted and that those using them are aware of the tentative nature of some of them.

It is in the light of these considerations that Finlay has delved into the contemporary scientific literature in some depth. While non-scientists may be tempted to skim over these sections or even bypass them altogether, that would be a loss. He analyses both reproductive and therapeutic (research) cloning, bringing out the scientific pros and cons of each. What emerges are the large number of unknowns, and the ever-changing issues that are inevitably present in any dynamic and exciting scientific field. This particular one is no different from any other in this regard. Then, against the background provided by this scientific analysis, he comments at some length on ethical and theological issues affecting the utilisation of stem cells. While he is not writing as a scientist *per se* in these sections, he is an interested observer writing within a broad Christian framework. Here he draws valuable distinctions between blastocysts (early embryos) arising from fertilisation and those arising from somatic cell nuclear transfer (SCNT), commenting in particular on the scientific distinctives of the two populations. The ethical conclusions he draws are obviously open to debate, and yet the scientific issues should be matters of general interest.

Finlay's reflections on theology and science bring to both areas the awareness of a scientist and the concerns of one committed to the Christian faith. His final section on wider ethical issues attempts to place the debate on stem cells and the protection of human embryos within the context of issues of justice and health priorities. This introduces questions regarding the costs of high-tech healthcare, the ease with which the needs of the poor are overlooked, and the deceptiveness of the temptation to believe that all diseases, let alone aging, are curable. Of course, these delusions affect the development of therapies involving adult stem cells as much as embryonic stem cells. Human dignity is as much at stake here as in debates on the human embryo.

Liz Hepburn reviews the challenges that arose in a court case relating to two frozen *in vitro* fertilisation (IVF) embryos 'orphaned' by the death of the couple they were conceived from. The outcome of the case depended on the status of the embryos. A cartoon of the time depicted the intense focus given to resolving this problem whilst ignoring the much larger plight of the many millions in the world suffering poverty, disease and starvation. Hepburn uses this cartoon to highlight two substantive issues of justice and health priorities and the status of the embryo and shows how they highlight a challenge to our humanity. Both legal and medical perspectives on the embryo are explored demonstrating an ongoing ambivalence about the status, derived from moral and legal protection, that we accord the embryo. Other philosophical positions also demonstrate the difficulty philosophically and scientifically of marking a point at which to attribute humanity and accord human rights.

Hepburn shows that an economic justice argument would point towards a focus on diseases that are more prevalent and require less intensive technology. However, the stronger point is the disengagement of theology with the realities of the world and our own experience. Such division, arising from a dualism and emphasis on objectivity enables us to debate the humanity of the yet-to-be embryo and ignore the humanity of millions of fellow human beings. Thus the status of the embryo and stem cell research cannot be separated from the broader question of how we are as humans in this world.

Ian Barns picks up on some of these points from a different perspective. His discussion looks at the influence of biomedical technologies on altering the very nature of human existence. Does the human race have a 'posthuman future', as Fukuyama has claimed? However, Barns is explicit in pointing out that these emerging technologies are not the only or even the most important changes that bring our humanness into question. There is a range of cultural and contextual factors that have led to profound shifts in our view of ourselves. These in turn have led to a variety of responses, from the techno-optimists to the civic humanists. But where, Barns asks, does a Christian view fit in?

To answer this question he expounds a post-Cartesian view of the human person. He seeks to provide a Christian account of human personhood within the context provided by the practices of Christian community. This starts with the central narrative of the Christian faith, namely, Jesus' life, death, resurrection, and ascension, and the manner in which this demonstrates what it means to be human. Against this background, he aims to work out the kind of ethical perspective on modern genetics that might follow from this. For instance, Barns considers that limits to scientific endeavours stem, not from an argument based on naturalness, but from the creational/eschatological logic of the gospel narrative. His approach also acknowledges a continuing tension and ambivalence towards human creativity, with its balance between demonic tendencies and God's grace.

Ultimately, what Barns comes back to is the centrality of Christian community. He sees a need for the church to develop practices of positive and critical discernment towards the emerging range of biotechnologies. The aim of all these should be enhancement of the common good, with its built-in communal and relational con-siderations. While these emphases do not provide cut-and-dried answers to specific issues associated with stem cell and cloning technologies, they place them within a helpful overarching Christian context.

Gareth Jones returns to more general scientific issues and commences with reflecting on whether theologians could have contributed more to the evolution of the current debate on stem cells and cloning. Any answer we give to this query may be relevant to any ongoing contributions we should or should not expect from them. Jones assesses at some length what he regards as dominating motifs in discussions on biotechnologies—playing God and designer babies. He considers that both are unhelpful simplifications of the issues at stake, and that their semi-religious overtones militate against constructive debate. The negative connotations with which they are most often depicted obscure the positive element implicit within the biblical picture that humans are to act as those created in the image of God. Why should humans as God's agents and stewards *not* act like God and *not* be involved in at least minor ways in designing human beings? The simple act of posing such a question can be seriously misinterpreted and can lead to intense opposition. Jones's aim is to work through the pros and cons of beginning to think in these ways.

Jones discusses reproductive and therapeutic cloning by analysing the arguments usually put forward in opposition to them. His emphasis is on those arguments having a theological rationale. This brings him face-to-face with the ambiguous status of the human embryo, especially when brought into existence within an artificial and therapeutic context, with the intention of benefiting patients and alleviating suffering. The relationship between scientific and theological considerations comes to the fore here, demonstrating the complexity of the interactions and the manner in which all sorts of assumptions may need to be revisited.

Similar considerations emerge in the realm of stem cells. What Jones also aims to bring out here is the manner in which social policy regulations have theological overtones. These regulations also have widespread implications for many other facets of healthcare. This observation reminds us that underlying every aspect of these discussions is the importance of the character of human beings as people before God and as people living in community.

Andrew Dutney further addresses the issue of stem cells. He begins with the position that stem cell research is not particularly controversial as the potential benefits justify the research. The most significant ethical debate is the source of the stem cells. Dutney shows that within the Christian community there is a range of views. At the Catholic end of the spectrum fertilisation is the point at which moral protection is afforded to all human beings. Alternatively the Anglican Archbishop of Perth recognises a human being fourteen days after fertilisation, as conception is a developmental process. Dutney allows the same time-frame but argues that implantation is the significant marker. This is the point of interaction between the mother and the embryo, the point at which the woman is considered pregnant. Many embryos do not implant and hence, not every embryo is the beginning of a human being.

Dutney shows that this is even more evident with embryos in the IVF process. Relating it to a theological anthropology Dutney shows that such an approach is grounded in the Trinitarian God, God who has being in relationship. Therefore, human life has being in relationship at the point of implantation. When this is applied to IVF embryos prior to implantation, they can be distinguished from embryos in utero, and may, respectfully, be used in research.

D Gareth Jones
Mary Byrne

Cloning and Stem Cells: Reflecting on the State of the Science

Graeme Finlay
Auckland

1.Introduction

Transplantation medicine has made use of donated tissues that are in limited supply, often immunologically incompatible with the recipient, and not always of desirable quality[1] (Figure 1). The option of growing cells or tissues to order is an attractive alternative, but has long been nothing more than a mere fantasy. The hope that such a strategy could be practicable has arisen recently from a new appreciation of the nature of stem cells. These are primitive cells with extensive regenerative potential that can differentiate into specialised tissue types (Table 1). Stem cells derived from early embryos are able to develop into essentially all the cell types that constitute the human body, and are said to be *pluripotent*. Those isolated from many organs in the body have the potential to develop into a more restricted range of cell types, and are designated as *multipotent*. The term *totipotent* refers to the ability to give rise to a complete individual, an ability possessed by the early embryo (blastocyst) within a woman's body.

In addition, the possibility has arisen that cells for tissue repair could be generated using the cloning technology that produced Dolly the sheep.[2] This involves the transfer of nuclei from normal somatic (body) cells into recipient oocytes that have had their own nuclei removed. Following such somatic cell nuclear transfer (SCNT), substances present in the oocyte trigger the reprogramming of the donated nucleus, and lead to the development of an early form of the embryo (a blastocyst). This blastocyst can be placed either into a uterus for reproductive purposes (*reproductive cloning*), or grown in culture for

---

1. A Vats, NS Tolley, JM Polak *et al*, 'Stem Cells: Sources and Applications', *Clinical Otolaryngology* 27 (2002): 227–232.
2. I Wilmut, AE Schneike, J McWhir *et al*, 'Viable Offspring Derived from Fetal and Adult Mammalian Cells', *Nature* 385 (1997): 810–813.

later recovery of embryonic stem cells (ESCs), from which specialised cells may be derived. Derivation of ESCs is the essential step which (it is hoped) will allow the generation of unlimited numbers of specified cell types for tissue repair. This process is known as *therapeutic cloning*[3] (Figure 2). Cloning technology is attractive because it would allow a patient's own cells to be reprogrammed to generate immunologically compatible replacements for diseased tissue.

The possibility of the reproductive cloning of humans has elicited universal condemnation. The possibility of therapeutic cloning has occasioned controversy for two reasons: it could be a step towards reproductive cloning; and it involves the destruction of human embryos. After considering the development of SCNT technology and some lessons arising from the reproductive cloning controversy, this discussion will address therapeutic cloning.

2. Reproductive cloning of totipotent stem cells: some lessons

The range of animal species that have been cloned reproductively reflects interest in laboratory models (mice, rats, rabbits) and farm animals of economic importance (sheep, goats, cattle, pigs, horses). Additional species are being cloned as technical difficulties are progressively solved.[4] Until recently, primate embryos could not be generated by SCNT, probably because primate oocytes possess an unusual arrangement of the mitotic spindle relative to the nucleus, leading to spindle damage when the nucleus is removed.[5] This was confirmed when nuclear extrusion from oocytes rather than fine needle aspiration led to the formation of human blastocysts.[6]

---

3. Cogle CR, Guthrie SM, Sanders RC *et al*, 'An Overview of Stem Cell Research and Regulatory Issues', *Mayo Clinic Proceedings* 78 (2003): 993–1003; R Lanza and N Rosenthal, 'The Stem Cell Challenge', *Scientific American* (2004): 92–99.

4. L Paterson, P De Sousa, W Ritchie *et al*, 'Application of Reproductive Biotechnology in Animals: Implications and Potentials. Applications of reproductive cloning', *Animal Reproductive Science* 79 (2003): 137–143.

5. SM Rhind, JE Taylor, PA De Sousa *et al*, 'Human Cloning: Can It Be Made Safe?', *Nature Reviews Genetics* 4 (2003): 855–864.

6. WS Hwang, YJ Ryu, JH Park *et al*, 'Evidence of a Pluripotent Human Embryonic Stem Cell Line Derived from a Cloned Blastocyst', *Science* 303 (2004): 1669–1674.

This highly acclaimed and controversial work was the first successful derivation of blastocysts and ESCs from adult human somatic cell nuclei. It increases the likelihood that reproductive and therapeutic cloning of primates will be achievable.

The possibility of reproductive cloning of humans has raised *ethical* concerns, chief among which is the fear that the personal act of procreation would be transformed into an impersonal 'species of manufacture'.[7] Additionally, the creation of life would occur beyond the boundaries of a loving parental relationship.[8] But in the fallenness of human society, the normal sexual conception of children is no guarantee of faithful and loving parental commitment, and many of the objections to reproductive cloning may well be equally applicable to the begetting of children by natural means.[9] For instance, can *stigmatisation* of cloned children be a consideration when stigmatisation (based on skin colour, skin blemishes or social class) is widespread and is in the eye of the beholder? With regard to the *instrumentalisation* of children, natural parents may see their children as status symbols, a source of security for old age, or objects manifesting their creativity. In relation to the *commodification* of human life, children have been commodified as workers on subsistence farms, as sweat labour in factories, or as objects in the sex industry. *A right to genetic uniqueness* cannot be justified, given that monozygotic twins are not genetically unique. The danger for all parents is to mould their children in their own image.

Concerns have also been expressed that reproductive cloning may legitimise despotic parental tendencies to predetermine the course of

7.   RP George, 'Human Cloning and Embryo Research: The 2003 John J Conley Lecture on Medical Ethics', *Theories of Medicine* 25 (2004): 3–20.

8.   C MacKellar, 'Creation—a Bond of Love (Debate)?', *Science and Christian Belief* 16 (2004): 50–53.

9.   F Watts, *Christians and Bioethics* (London: SPCK, 2000); DG Jones, 'Human Cloning: Unwarranted Control or Legitimate Stewardship?', *Science and Christian Belief* 14 (2002): 159–180.

their children's lives.[10] Alongside this, it may represent the arrogation of inappropriate control over those yet to be born.[11]

Nevertheless, such concerns are not intrinsic to the *means* of conception, but to the *value* in which children are held. The issue is not the mechanics of child-production, but the nurturing environment of love, care and discipline into which children (however they may be conceived) are born.[12] On the other hand, the current existence of gross abuses of children does not provide justification for introducing innovative technology, if that technology entails those abuses as an intrinsic feature of its operation.

Jones[13] expresses the fear that objections to reproductive cloning based on the Christian story can easily be presented as (or interpreted as) knee-jerk opposition to biomedical technology. To address this danger, it is important to realise that: all informed people of goodwill and integrity will not necessarily agree on ethical issues; the specificity of Christian ethics is based on the stories of God's creative and redemptive commitment to his world; Christians cannot expect others to perceive or appreciate the weight of their perspectives. Consequently, Christians have a responsibility to explain their perspectives without seeking to enforce them on others.

A compelling *pragmatic* reason for proscribing human reproductive cloning is that the approach is inherently unsafe. It is associated with very low efficiencies (live births/implanted blastocyst), increased frequencies of spontaneous abortions and neonatal deaths, poorly understood pathologies, and abnormalities in the manner in which genes are regulated.[14] This is because genetic systems themselves are regulated through epigenetic marking, that is, chemical tagging of DNA and its associated proteins. Such epigenetic marking occurs differentially on the maternally- and paternally-derived chromosomes,

---

10. F Bowring, 'Therapeutic and Reproductive Cloning: A Critique', in *Social Science and Medicine* 58 (2004): 401–409.

11. N Messer, 'Cloning, Creation and Control (Debate)', *Science and Christian Belief* 16 (2004): 45–50.

12. Cogle, 'An Overview of Stem Cell Research and Regulatory Issues', *op cit*.

13. Jones, 'Human Cloning: Unwarranted Control or Legitimate Stewardship?' *op cit*; DG Jones, 'A Response by Gareth Jones (Debate)', *Science and Christian Belief* 16 (2004): 53–55.

14. Rhind, 'Human Cloning: Can It Be Made Safe?', *op cit*.

thereby highlighting what could be a major obstacle to normal development in cloning.

Even the now standard assisted reproductive technologies (ARTs), such as *in vitro* fertilisation (IVF) and intracytoplasmic sperm injection (ICSI), are associated with a higher incidence of diseases.[15] Multiple pregnancies arising from ART is an important risk factor, but even with single births the frequencies of premature delivery, reduced birth weight, perinatal mortality and major birth defects may be increased.[16]

The use of ART in farm animals produces a high frequency of abnormally large calves and lambs manifesting a spectrum of abnormalities ('large offspring syndrome'). While these conditions may arise from components of the culture systems used for embryo propagation, their immediate cause is abnormal epigenetic regulation of the genetic program.[17]

Reproductive cloning is seen by wide-eyed techno-utopians as a means to improve society by manipulating 'biologically/genetically determined' behaviour and intelligence,[18] but is rejected universally by scientists[19] and legislators.[20] It would represent a unique form of experimentation. Reproductive cloning would amount to a procedure in which the *people* were the experiment, the outcome of which could not be known until they were shown to possess the capacity of producing normal children.

---

15.   GF Cox, J Burger, V Lip *et al*, 'Intracytoplasmic Sperm Injection May Increase The Risk of Imprinting Defects', *American Journal of Human Genetics* 71 (2002): 162–164; AC Moll, SM Imhof, JRM Cruysberg *et al*, 'Incidence of Retinoblastoma in Children Born after In-vitro Fertilization', *Lancet* 361 (2003): 309–310.

16.   See Rhind, 'Human Cloning: Can It Be Made Safe?', *op cit.*

17.   EL Niemitz and AP Feinberg, 'Epigenetics and Assisted Reproductive Technology: A Call for Investigation', *American Journal of Human Genetics* 74 (2004): 599–609.

18.   SW Itzkoff, 'Intervening with Mother Nature: The Ethics of Human Cloning', *The Mankind Quarterly* XLIV/1 (2003): 29–42.

19.   Rhind, 'Human Cloning: Can It Be Made Safe?', *op cit.*

20.   I Nippert, 'The Pros and Cons of Human Therapeutic Cloning in the Public Debate', *Journal of Biotechnology* 98 (2002): 53–60.

3. Therapeutic cloning: pluripotent stem cells

A possible approach to repairing damaged organs is to grow custom-made cells. These would be derived from primitive cells that possess both an unlimited capacity for proliferation and the ability to mature into any one of the cell types comprising the human body. Early blastocysts contain ESCs with the necessary properties (Figure 2), since ESCs can differentiate *in vitro* and *in vivo* into all the specialised cell types of the human body. They are pluripotential.

IVF. Using IVF, only those blastocysts excess to requirements for fertility treatment would be available. Embryos generated by IVF are not ideal as a therapeutic strategy because each derived ESC line possesses a unique combination of cell surface proteins. Hence, they are immunologically incompatible with potential recipients.

SCNT. This procedure, using oocytes as recipients of nuclei (Figure 2), remains the one proven method of re-setting the developmental clock of an adult nucleus.[21] The advantages of a SCNT approach are that a patient's own cells would be cloned, so avoiding the problems of incompatibility.

Despite the high expectations, Mombaerts[22] has warned that few groups have described therapeutic cloning. The full sequence of events has only been achieved by a few research teams in mice and by one in humans (Table 2). Remarkable proof-of-principle studies in the mouse have demonstrated the *in vitro* generation of specified types of cells (Figure 3).

The achievement of Hwang[23] in using SCNT to generate a human ESC line may have resulted from the extrusion (rather than the aspiration) of the oocyte nucleus, and the optimisation of culture conditions. The ESC line has a normal chromosome complement and can differentiate into multiple cell types representing all three germ layers. Even so, the very low efficiency of deriving ESC lines suggests the presence of underlying abnormalities in the huge majority of blastocysts. Transfers using only nuclei of cumulus cells and oocytes from the same woman were successful. Transfers using nuclei from males did not even give blastocysts.

---

21. P Mombaerts, 'Therapeutic Cloning in the Mouse', *Proceedings of the National Academy of Sciences USA* 100 (2003): 11924–11925.

22. *Ibid.*

23. Hwang, 'Evidence of a Pluripotent Human Embryonic Stem Cell Line Derived from a Cloned Blastocyst', *op cit.*

The weight of utilitarian arguments in favour of proceeding with SCNT technology depends on the healthcare benefits that will accrue. According to Wilmut,[24] 'cloning promises such great benefits that it would be immoral not to do it'. He cites as important benefits the ability to study diseases for which events early in pathogenesis cannot otherwise be investigated, and the development of therapies (including those rectifying inherited diseases). Similarly, Holm[25] concludes that 'the very large and very likely benefits of stem cell research indicate that prohibition of stem cell research needs strong justification'. A more sober assessment is provided by Shannon[26] who writes, 'Embryonic stem cell therapy is at present a promissory note, a scientific hypothesis, and a claim to be established.'

What, then, is the status of the technology? Oocytes are scarce,[27] insufficient even for ongoing IVF procedures. This may ultimately preclude their use in therapeutic cloning.[28] It follows that, in most countries, oocytes are expensive (US$1,000–2,000 each). The situation is different in South Korea, where oocytes are obtainable without remuneration to the donor. Even here the ethical situation is sensitive, as evinced by the furore that erupted after the ESC cloning breakthrough.[29] The danger of oocytes being a saleable commodity raises concern that women could be pressurised or exploited, and that conflicts of interest could affect female researchers.[30]

Derivation of ESC lines by nuclear transfer remains inefficient (100 oocytes/ESC line). At current efficiencies, the oocyte bill would be a prohibitive US$100,000–200,000 for each customised line.

---

24. I Wilmut, 'The Moral Imperative for Human Cloning', *New Scientist* (21 February, 2004): 16–17.

25. A Holm, 'Going to the Roots of the Stem Cell Controversy', *Bioethics* 16 (2002): 493–507.

26. TA Shannon, 'Human Embryonic Stem Cell Therapy', *Theological Studies* 62 (2001): 811–824.

27. D Solter, 'New Paths to ES Cells?', *Nature Biotechnology* 21 (2003): 1154–1155.

28. ME Coors, 'Therapeutic Cloning: From Consequences to Contradiction', *Journal of Medicine and Philosophy* 27 (2002): 297–317.

29. Hwang, 'Evidence of a Pluripotent Human Embryonic Stem Cell Line Derived from a Cloned Blastocyst', *op cit.*

30. A McLaren, 'Ethical and Social Considerations of Stem Cell Research', *Nature* 414 (2001): 129–131.

Unfortunately, there is little hope in achieving the efficiency required to make nuclear transfer-based therapeutic cloning a practicable proposition in the near future.

Much about ESC biology remains unknown. The effect of prolonged culture on the chromosome complement[31] (and on pluripotency) remains uncertain. ESCs may contain rare 'cancer stem cells' and have a tendency to generate tumours such as teratomas; they may also differentiate into unwanted cell types.[32] There have been unanticipated problems in achieving successful engraftment in experimental animals. For instance, difficulties in transplanting ESC-derived blood cell progenitors into genetically matched recipient mice may arise because low expression of proteins on cell surfaces may induce rejection by natural killer cells.[33]

Due to the daunting technical difficulties, Mombaerts[34] sees the need to discover alternative approaches to somatic cell cloning for therapy. Hypothetical alternatives are presented in the 'possibility map' of Figure 1, in that it may be possible to induce the development of oocytes from cultured ESCs, as has been shown for murine ESCs.[35] Oocytes from cows or rabbits may be used as recipients of human cell-derived nuclei, although mitochondrial proteins encoded by genes in the human nucleus may not be compatible with the mitochondria of the host oocyte.[36] Imaginable oocyte-independent systems include fusing somatic cell nuclei with enucleated ESCs, and injecting 'reprogramming factors' into somatic cells to convert them into ESC-

31.   MF Pera, 'Unnatural Selection of Cultured Human ES Cells?', *Nature Biotechnology* 22 (2004): 42–43.
32.   Lanza, 'The Stem Cell Challenge', *op cit.*
33.   WM Rideout, K Hochedlinger, M Kyba *et al*, 'Correction of a Genetic Defect by Nuclear Transplantation and Combined Gene Therapy', *Cell* 109 (2002):17–27.
34.   Mombaerts, 'Therapeutic Cloning in the Mouse', *op cit.*
35.   K Hubner, G Fuhrmann, LK Christenson *et al*, 'Derivation of Oocytes from Mouse Embryonic Stem Cells', *Science* 300 (2003): 1251–1256.
36.   KH Chang, JM Lim, SK Kang *et al*, 'Blastocyst Formation, Karyotype, and Mitochondrial DNA of Interspecies Embryos Derived from Nuclear Transfer of Human Cord Fibroblasts into Enucleated Bovine Oocytes', *Fertility and Sterility* 80 (2003): 1380–1387; Solter, 'New Paths to ES Cells?', *op cit.*

like products.[37] That such approaches are being considered indicates the primitive state of the field.

4. Ethical issues

The creation of nuclear transfer-derived ESC lines remains controversial. There is no consensus in our pluralistic society regarding the moral status of the human embryo,[38] no new arguments are being presented, and the issue is considered irresolvable.[39] At one pole, the human embryo is seen to be a human person, while at the other it is seen as a mere collection of cells that 'does not have any interests to be protected'.[40] A mediating position recognises the embryo as a potential human being worthy of profound respect, and of increasing protection as development proceeds,[41] although the notion of 'respecting that which one destroys' seems incoherent to many people.[42]

Some would proscribe embryo research for therapeutic cloning because it represents a 'slippery slope' leading inexorably to reproductive cloning[43] in that successful SCNT for therapeutic purposes would make it easier and more tempting to attempt reproductive cloning.[44] However, *any* technical innovation might constitute an incremental movement on a slippery slope to a potential abuse. In a social context, the 'slippery slope' argument expresses the fear that SCNT for therapy will 'trivialise the use of embryos and ultimately dehumanise society'.[45] However, the tolerance shown by

---

37.   C Dennis, 'Take a Cell, Any cell . . .', *Nature* 426 (2003): 490–491.

38.   G Frazzetto, 'Embryos, Cells and God', *EMBO Rep* 5 (2004): 553–555.

39.   MJ Reiss, 'Ethical Dimensions of Therapeutic Human Cloning', *Journal of Biotechnology* 98 (2002): 61–70.

40.   Nippert, 'The Pros and Cons of Human Therapeutic Cloning in the Public Debate', *op cit.*

41.   DG Jones, 'The Human Embryo: Between Oblivion and Meaningful Life', *Science and Christian Belief* 6 (1994): 3-19; Shannon, 'Human Embryonic Stem Cell Therapy', *op cit.*

42.   Reiss, 'Ethical Dimensions of Therapeutic Human Cloning', *op cit.*

43.   Watts, *Christians and Bioethics, op cit.*

44.   Holm, 'Going to the Roots of the Stem Cell Controversy', *op cit.*

45.   Nippert, 'The Pros and Cons of Human Therapeutic Cloning in the Public Debate', *op cit.*

society to childhood poverty and abuse has more to do with dehumanisation than the activities in a culture laboratory.

In order to circumvent the black-and-white nature of so much discussion on what can be done to and with human embryos, Holm[46] has produced a suggested order of increasing ethical difficulty in the use of human tissue. According to this, the gradation is from the use of adult stem cells through two intermediate categories to the use of embryonic stem cells from nuclear transfer.

> 1. adult stem cells
>
> 2. embryonic stem cells from spare embryos (fertilised)
>
> 3. embryonic stem cells from embryos created for research (fertilised)
>
> 4. embryonic stem cells from nuclear transfer (SCNT)

While this gradation may not be obvious to everyone, it raises two considerations. Can the status of the blastocyst be clarified? Do blastocysts derived by fertilisation have the same status as those derived by SCNT?

4.1 The status of the blastocyst

There has been interminable discussion as to when a human being emerges or when personhood commences. Insights from the evolutionary development of the human species teach us that the *process* by which an embryo develops, no less than the final *product,* is the work of God. We have moved from the Aristotelian to an evolutionary world picture.[47]

Thus the spectrum of development from zygote to adulthood itself reflects an act of creation (Psalm139:13–16). Biblically, feotuses are recognised 'as an essential part on the continuum that makes up the prenatal and postnatal facets of human lives'[48] and this gives to every stage of the continuum the utmost value. Strict definitions of what 'human being' and 'personhood' mean, or where they start, are not helpful or necessary. The process from start to finish is a creative act of God. It elicits our awe and demands our reverent protection. Perhaps (to use the categories of Greek thought), it is more biblical to refer to us as 'human becomings' than 'human beings'. On this basis, human IVF

---

46.   Holm, 'Going to the Roots of the Stem Cell Controversy', *op cit.*

47.   Shannon, 'Human Embryonic Stem Cell Therapy', *op cit.*

48.   Jones, 'The Human Embryo: Between Oblivion and Meaningful Life', *op cit.*

embryos (Holm's categories 2 and 3) may be inappropriate for research or therapy, and every effort should be made to avoid the production of spare embryos.[49]

The specificity of the Christian story resides in recognising ourselves as created in the 'image of God' (Genesis1:26f), as seeing human development *in utero* as the creative work of the immanent ever-working God (for example, Jeremiah 1:5; Galatians 1:15), and as accepting that the incarnation of the Son of God in human flesh sanctifies the developmental spectrum of life (Luke1:31–32).

However, in a postmodern society there are no knock-down arguments by which Christians can compel others to adopt their ethical positions.[50] Ultimately, ethics do not come from rationally defensible propositions, but from the stories by which we are formed[51]. Perhaps Christians should rejoice in their own valuation of the gift of life and be prepared to forgo activities that would destroy human IVF-derived blastocysts, without demanding that society at large accept their story. But if this is the choice that Christians make, they must be prepared to forgo any of the medical benefits that arise from destruction of IVF embryos. For to enjoy the benefits of ESC technology is to legitimate the ethos according to which blastocysts are dismembered.[52]

4.2 Blastocysts arising from fertilisation and from SCNT

It seems reductionistic (even in narrowly scientific terms) and inaccurate to define new people in terms of their novel genetic constitutions or genetic potential. It requires much more than a genetic sequence to specify the route from zygote to adult. A DNA sequence cannot allow direct entry to, and traversal of, the developmental continuum in the absence of the appropriate pattern of regulation established by the epigenetic machinery.

Epigenetic factors distinct from genetic inheritance direct the development of certain cells into tumours of reproductive tissue rather

---

49.   MD Beer, *Christian Choices in Healthcare* (Leicester: IVP/CMF, 1995).

50.   Frazzetto, 'Embryos, Cells and God', *op cit.*

51.   S Hauerwas, *Vision and Virtue* (Notre Dame: University of Notre Dame Press, 1981).

52.   *contra* RM Green, 'Benefiting from "Evil": An Incipient Moral Problem in Human Stem Cell Research', *Bioethics* 16 (2002): 544–556.

than into people,[53] prevent parthenogenetic development,[54] and severely limit the development of SCNT zygotes (Table 3). Hydatidiform moles, ovarian teratomas, parthenogenetic embryos, and SCNT-derived embryos may well possess the genetic potential to develop into a baby because all the required genes are present. However, these structures are prevented from doing so by epigenetic constraints. SCNT-derived blastocysts retain features of somatic cells, and show abnormal epigenetic regulation and gene expression, particularly of the extra-embryonic trophectoderm—the support tissues.[55] SCNT blastocysts may also lack vital information in the form of messenger RNA contributed by sperm cells.[56]

A blastocyst derived by fertilisation is thus different from one derived by SCNT. The former has high potential to develop beyond the embryonic stage (twenty to thirty per cent[57]); the latter has exceedingly low potential. SCNT blastocysts (Holm's category 4), like their parthenogenetic counterparts, are essentially unprotectable embryos[58] displaced from the developmental continuum. They may represent merely artifactual extensions of the tissue of the nuclear donor. Harvest of SCNT blastocyts (day five) for recovery of ESCs would preclude the experimental manipulation of later stages (gastrulation, implantation, placentation) required for the realisation of authentic developmental potential.[59]

In view of these considerations, it is interesting to consider George's[60] contention that embryos possess the 'epigenetic primordia' for self-directed growth and maturation to adulthood. This may be

53. AP Feinberg and B Tycko, 'The History of Cancer Epigenetics', *Nature Reviews Cancer* 4 (2004): 143–153.
54. T Kono, Y Obata, Q Wu *et al*, 'Birth of Parthenogenetic Mice That Can Develop to Adulthood', *Nature* 428 (2004): 860–864.
55. A Jouneau and J-P Renard, 'Reprogramming in Nuclear Transfer', *Current Opinion on Genetics and Development* 13 (2003): 486–491.
56. GC Ostermeier, D Miller, JD Huntriss *et al*, 'Delivering Spermatozoan RNA to the Oocyte', *Nature* 429 (2004): 154.
57. Beer, *Christian Choices in Healthcare, op cit*
58. Jones, 'The Human Embryo: Between Oblivion and Meaningful Life', *op cit.*
59. Jouneau, 'Reprogramming in Nuclear Transfer', *op cit.*
60. George, 'Human Cloning and Embryo Research: The 2003 John J Conley Lecture on Medical Ethics', *op cit.*

true for blastocysts derived by fertilisation, but not SCNT blastocyts. The latter may thus be legitimate *in vitro* models, having no claim on the considerations that lead us to value 'human becomings' as creatures of God.

But what of the possibility that SCNT or reprogramming technology will one day enable the routine production of blastocysts from somatic cells? Such blastocysts might be shown (from experiments on other species) to have high developmental potential. The considerations developed above would then be superseded, and all such cloned blastocysts may be beyond manipulation. A branch of epigenetics research would be off-limits. Alternatively, it seems reductionistic to assert that the introduction of a few purified enzymes or messenger RNA species (that transform them to cystic structures containing pluripotential stem cells) into simple cells like fibroblasts represents an absolute boundary between disposable somatic cells and inviolable human beings. Is the difference between a mere collection of patients' cells and 'human becomings' really determined by so minimalist a procedure? Or might we look to a wider network of relationships to distinguish a blastocyst derived from a reprogrammed fibroblast from a blastocyst generated by the fusion of two gametes? It may be that the former cloned structure is not derivative from, and continuous with, a pre-existing person (Table 4). If our humanity rests not merely in our biology taken in isolation, but also in the network of relationships in which we live,[61] then could we say that the status of a blastocyst is determined within the human context in which it is produced? Could the very ethical considerations that proscribe reproductive use of a cloned blastocyst (Section 1) thereby legitimate its use for therapy?

5. Repair without cloning: multipotent adult stem cells

Another developing paradigm has major implications for regenerative medicine, that is, the adult body maintains populations of stem cells. These lack the pluripotentiality of ESCs, but retain the ability to develop into a variety of specialised cell types. If adult stem cells could be harnessed for tissue repair, the more technically demanding and controversial project of using SCNT to create ESCs would become unnecessary.

---

61. NG Messer, 'Human Genetics and the Image of the Triune God', *Science and Christian Belief* 13 (2001): 99.

Experiments in rodents have indicated that stem cell populations exist in many adult tissues and are replenished by precursors derived from the bone marrow (BM). For example, experimental perturbation of blood sugar concentrations leads to the generation of BM-derived pro-insulin-expressing cells in several tissues.[62] However, the development of primitive precursor cells into various types of specialised cells has not been universally demonstrated. The diversity of results has been attributed to experimental variables, such as the age of recipient mice, the presence of injury in recipient mice, and the strain of donor mice.[63]

In humans, circulating stem cells may replenish specialised cell populations in many organs. This suggestion has arisen through strategies based on the ability to distinguish cells from male and female individuals by the presence of the male-specific Y chromosome. The appearance of Y chromosome-containing cells in organs transplanted from females into males demonstrates that precursors from the recipient migrate into the organs and differentiate. Transplants of haematopoietic cells from males into females indicate that the male-derived blood cells contribute to many specialised cell types.[64] A universal stem cell may roam throughout the body, taking up residence wherever it is needed to promote regeneration. Even the heart and brain (classically considered to be non-regenerating) may undergo some degree of repopulation.

BM stem cells can form a wider spectrum of specialised cell types than was suspected a few years ago (Figure 3). The mesenchymal stem

62. H Kojima, M Fujimiya, K Nakahara *et al*, 'Extrahepatic Insulin-producing Cells in Multiple Organs in Diabetes', *Proceedings of the National Academy of Sciences USA* 101 (2004): 2458–2463.

63. DJ Prockop, CA Gregory and JL Spees, 'One Strategy for Cell and Gene Therapy: Harnessing the Power of Adult Stem Cells to Repair Tissues', *Proceedings of the National Academy of Sciences USA* 100 (2003): 11917–11923.

64. W Kleeberger, A Versmold, T Rothamel *et al* 'Increased Chimerism of Bronchial and Alveolar Epithelium in Lung Allografts Undergoing Chronic Injury', *American Journal of Pathology* 162 (2003): 1487–1494.

cell (MSC) population readily expanded from rodent[65] and human[66] marrow is a promising candidate that could be used for tissue repair[67] and engineering,[68] and as a vehicle for rectifying gene defects.[69] BM stem cells are multipotential, readily available, greatly expandable in culture, genetically compatible with the donor (so avoiding problems with rejection), and do not have a tendency to form tumours. They can be prepared without the problems of supply and technical sophistication that limit SCNT application. Whether BM-derived MSCs are able to repair tissue injury is under active study.

Products of bone-derived cells[70] induce human MSC differentiation into mineralised osteogenic cells *in vitro*. The potential of MSCs to rectify bone disease has been shown by culturing MSCs from patients with the genetic disease osteogenesis imperfecta, eliminating the causative gene, and transplanting MSC-derived osteogenic cells into mice where they formed bone.[71]

The conversion of human BM cells to muscle cells occurs readily *in vitro*. Human BM cells injected into damaged muscles in mice differentiate into muscle cells (providing 0.1–0.2% of the muscle cell population). Muscles engineered to express a locally acting growth

65. L da Silva Meirelles and NB Nardi, 'Murine Marrow-derived Mesenchymal Stem Cells: Isolation, *in vitro* Expansion, and Characterisation', *British Journal of Haematology* 123 (2003): 702–711.

66. Prockop, 'One Strategy for Cell and Gene Therapy: Harnessing the Power of Adult Stem Cells to Repair Tissues', *op cit.*

67. A Musaro, C Giacinti, G Borsellino *et al*, 'Stem Cell-mediated Muscle Regeneration is Enhanced by Local Isoform of Insulin-like Growth Factor 1', *Proceedings of the National Academy of Sciences USA* 101 (2004): 1206–1210.

68. XB Yang, DW Green, HI Roach, 'Novel Osteoinductive Biomimetic Scaffolds Stimulate Human Osteoprogenitor Activity: Implications for Skeletal Repair', *Connective Tissue Research* 44/S1 (2003): 312–317.

69. JR Chamberlain, U Schwarze, P-R Wang *et al*, 'Gene Targeting in Stem Cells from Individuals with Osteogenesis Imperfecta', *Science* 303 (2004): 1198–1201.

70. Yang, 'Novel Osteoinductive Biomimetic Scaffolds Stimulate Human Osteoprogenitor Activity: Implications for Skeletal Repair', *op cit.*

71. Chamberlain, 'Gene Targeting in Stem Cells from Individuals with Osteogenesis Imperfecta', *op cit.*

factor showed an enhanced ability to recruit BM stem cells and direct their myogenic conversion in damaged sites.[72]

Adult multipotent stem cells may be recovered from other tissues also. Cells from *brain* and *skeletal muscle* can reconstitute BM in experimental animals.[73] Stem cells resident in muscle differentiate into muscle fibres when appropriately cultured, and can differentiate into muscle cells and fuse with pre-existing fibres if inoculated into mice with muscular dystrophy. For example, elucidation of the signals that recruit circulating precursor cells to damaged muscle offers hope for treatment of Duchenne muscular dystrophy.[74] Stem cells in rodent[75] but not human[76] brain continuously generate neurons. Since the human brain may resist the interpolation of nascent neurons into existing networks,[77] this could be a major impediment to achieving repair of damaged brain.

As shown in Table 5, many basic scientific questions regarding the reconstitution of functional tissue within major lesions, such as coronary infarcts, remain unanswered. Consequently, as Rosenthal[78] has argued, the future of adult stem cell-mediated therapies depends on the resolution of a host of unknowns.

6. Reflecting on theology

Christian theology seeks to integrate all human experience within the world-view of biblical faith. Its scope includes issues on which the

---

72. Musaro, 'Stem cell-mediated Muscle Regeneration is Enhanced by Local Isoform of Insulin-like Growth Factor 1', *op cit.*

73. N Rosenthal, 'Prometheus's Vulture and the Stem Cell Promise', *New England Journal of Medicine* 349 (2003): 267–274.

74. E Bachrach, S Li, AL Perez *et al*, 'Systemic Delivery of Human Microdystrophin to Regenerating Mouse Dystrophic Muscle by Muscle Progenitor Cells', *Proceedings of the National Academy of Sciences USA* 101 (2004): 3581–3586.

75. F Doetsch, 'A Niche for Adult Neural Stem Cells', *Current Opinion on Genetics and Development* 13 (2003): 543–550.

76. N Sanai, AD Tramontin, A Quinones-Hinojosa *et al*, 'Unique Astrocyte Ribbon in Adult Human Brain Contains Neural Stem Cells but Lacks Chain Migration', *Nature* 427 (2004): 740-744, 590.

77. P Rakic, 'Immigration Denied', *Nature* 427 (2004): 685–686.

78. Rosenthal, 'Prometheus's Vulture and the Stem Cell Promise', *op cit.*

Bible may seem ambiguous because of its originating milieu (slavery), or is necessarily silent (global warming, biotechnology).

Human creativity and ingenuity will always present Christians with novel, unanticipated and surprising perspectives on reality. The discoveries of the heliocentric universe, the geological time-frame, and the evolution of life demanded reappraisal of long-standing theological traditions. It can be argued, therefore, that Christians are to seek to 'renew and refresh' their world-view (rooted as it is in Scripture, tradition, reason and religious experience) 'by contact with the methods and descriptions of science'.[79] To fulfill this role, theology requires a listening attitude.

There is a need for continual awareness. With the inexorable march of human discovery and inventiveness, theology necessarily awaits new developments. Science and technology set the agenda. The cloning of Dolly from a somatic cell of an adult sheep[80] caught even eminent scientists by surprise. No less revolutionary have been the creation of parthenogenetic mice (derived from a maternal genome),[81] and the discovery of neural stem cells in the brains of adult mammals.[82]

There is a need for acute attentiveness. Science is a Christian way of thinking. Christians must therefore welcome its findings with the utmost seriousness. This requires the humility of submitting to the facts. Regarding therapeutic cloning, a 'bioethical analysis that ignores or distorts pertinent science is either uninformed or disingenuous. It is critical to understand the science correctly in order to assess the ethical issues correctly and draw good conclusions'.[83] Christians must also show scrupulous honesty in assessing issues and must not be seen as the reactionary instigators of a new 'science versus religion' conflict.[84]

---

79. C Southgate, C Deane-Drummond, PD Murray *et al*, *God, Humanity and the Cosmos* (Harrisburg: Pennsylvania, 1999).
80. Wilmut, 'Viable Offspring Derived from Fetal and Adult Mammalian Cells', *op cit*.
81. Kono, 'Birth of Parthenogenetic Mice That Can Develop to Adulthood', *op cit*.
82. Doetsch, 'A Niche for Adult Neural Stem Cells', *op cit*.
83. Coors, 'Therapeutic Cloning: From Consequences to Contradiction', *op cit*.
84. Frazzetto, 'Embryos, Cells and God', *op cit*.

There is a need for thoughtful discrimination. Christians must be alert to media-amplified distortions of cloning stories,[85] such as those emanating from science-fiction religious cults. Hall[86] laments the over-reaction to sensationalised (often unsubstantiated) claims, the absence of critical judgment in assessing these claims, and the devaluation of science in the discussion. The ethical implications of stem cell research are indeed too important to be left to scientists alone. However, the science behind stem cell research is too important to be abused by society's non-scientific ideologues. Critical judgment is vital.

There is a need for the church to show confidence in its role. Scientists *qua* scientists cannot speak with authority on ethical issues. Science has no language or conception of value. 'Science alone cannot dictate right or wrong in a moral sense or comment on the good for humankind. Science determines what can be done, not what should be done.'[87]

Considerations of value must be imported from elsewhere into discussions on the value of human life, the status of the embryo, or the relative priorities awarded to biomedical goals. Not everything that is technically possible is right.

Christian moral theology is to assesses innovations in technology in terms of its deepest motivations. It should not so much appeal to laws, precepts, or principles, as to faithfulness to the formative story of God's action in the world.[88] The mission of Christians is to care for others, especially the weak, and to mediate God's work of healing and renewal, so that 'any modifications of nature that we undertake should be ones that are consistent with what we discern to be the creative purposes of God'.[89] This affirms a strong deontological component to Christian bioethics. Considerations are inherently right/wrong in addition to being good/bad (utilitarian). Indeed, narrowly utilitarian

85. PD Hopkins, 'Bad Copies: How Popular Media Represent Cloning as an Ethical Problem', *Hastings Centre Report* (March-April 1988): 6–13.

86. SS Hall, 'Eve Redux: The Public Confusion over Cloning', *Hastings Center Report* 33 (2003): 11–15.

87. Coors, 'Therapeutic Cloning: From Consequences to Contradiction', *op cit.*

88. Hauerwas, *Vision and Virtue, op cit.*

89. Watts, *Christians and Bioethics, op cit.*

reasoning is inadequate when the nature and status of humanness are being assessed.[90]

7. Reflecting on science

The work of scientists must be understood, but their pronouncements do not carry final authority. Scientists may push personal (tacit) agendas. Much of the justification for gene therapy was based on its value to sufferers of (rare) genetic disorders. However, most projects were in fact directed towards common diseases, the treatment of which would be commercially viable.[91] People with rare genetic disorders were exploited to gain political and public acceptance of gene therapy approaches from which they could not expect to benefit. Promises of SCNT-based therapeutic advances may on occasions legitimate cherished research programs, including those that generate patentable products.[92]

Scientists may present selectively data that give support to their particular *a priori* position ('cherry-picking'[93]). Protagonists of reproductive cloning promote the idea of screening embryos prior to implantation even though the range and nature of epigenetic effects for which screening might be undertaken are unknown. Conversely, supporters of adult stem cell use have suppressed evidence pointing to their inadequacy.[94]

Scientists can be over-enthusiastic. A *Nature* editorial, commenting on the original Dolly paper, predicted that reproductive cloning would be possible in 'one to ten years'.[95] It took seven years to generate cloned human blastocysts, a mere first step towards reproductive cloning. Holm[96] warns that the promise of real, huge and immediate benefits within five to ten years will not be fulfilled, and cites the disappointments of gene therapy as a warning. The failure to deliver

---

90. Coors, 'Therapeutic Cloning: From Consequences to Contradiction', *op cit*; G Chu, 'Embryonic Stem-cell Research and the Moral Status of Embryos', *International Medical Journal* 33 (2003): 530–531.

91. Holm, 'Going to the Roots of the Stem Cell Controversy', *op cit.*

92. Bowring, 'Therapeutic and Reproductive Cloning: A Critique', *op cit.*

93. Rhind, 'Human Cloning: Can It Be Made Safe?', *op cit.*

94. E Blackburn and J Rowley, 'Reason as Our Guide', *PLoS Biology* 2 (2004): 420–422.

95. Editorial, 'Caught Napping by Clones', *Nature* 385 (1997): 753.

96. Holm, 'Going to the Roots of the Stem Cell Controversy', *op cit.*

on many promises calls for sober assessment of biotechnological claims. The potential long-term benefits of therapeutic cloning do not mandate unrestrained development of the technology.

Scientists are often divided. There is disagreement whether the preferred source of cells for embryo research should be fetal tissue and spare IVF embryos (favoured in the USA) or SCNT products (preferred in the UK [97]), while the relative merits of SCNT and adult stem cell approaches are debated.[98] The question of whether stem cells should be considered for replacement or merely for trophic protection is open.[99] For instance, the ability of adult haematopoietic stem cells to generate cardiomyocytes[100] and the role of cell fusion[101] are unresolved questions.

Scientists cannot predict the future of stem cell technologies. What somatic cells are best for SCNT? Cumulus cells (available only from females) and adult marrow MSCs[102] have been used, but the field is open. What must be stressed is that 'this research remains in its infancy . . . to put the debate into an accurate scientific context it is necessary to emphasise how very preliminary is the current work.'[103] The therapeutic goal will remain distant until much more is known about the basic molecular mechanisms that are involved in nuclear reprogramming.[104]

---

97. *Ibid.*

98. Blackburn and J Rowley, 'Reason as Our Guide', *op cit.*

99. CN Svendsen and JW Langston, 'Stem Cells for Parkinson Disease and ALS: Replacement or Protection?', *Nature Medicine* 10 (2004): 224–225.

100. CE Murry, MH Soonpaa, H Reineke *et al*, 'Haematopoietic Stem Cells Do Not Transdifferentiate into Cardiac Myocytes in Myocardial Infarcts', *Nature* 428 (2004): 664–668.

101. JM Nygren, S Jovinge, M Breitbach *et al*, 'Bone Marrow-derived Haematopoietic Cells Generate Cardiomyocytes at a Low Frequency Through Cell Division, but Not Transdifferentiation', *Nature Medicine* 10 (2004): 494–501.

102. Y Kato, H Imabayashi, T Mori *et al*, 'Nuclear Transfer of Adult Bone Marrow Mesenchymal Stem Cells: Developmental Totipotency of Tissue-specific Stem Cells from an Adult Mammal', *Biology of Reproduction* 70 (2004): 415–418.

103. Shannon, 'Human embryonic stem cell therapy', *op cit.*

8. Reflecting on the wider ethical issues

Justice in allocating limited resources. Even if therapeutic cloning was achievable technically, it would be very expensive and hence only available for the very rich.[105] In similar vein, Shannon[106] warns that 'Research initiatives such as stem cell therapy continue to replicate the dominant trend of high tech, high cost rescue medicine . . . the focus will continue to be on cure rather than prevention . . . ' At issue is not merely the ethics of ESC research but the very system of high tech healthcare, particularly the one that is dominant in the United States. The poor are not likely to benefit. A critical issue remains general access to healthcare. Cloning is limited to the generation of cells for a particular individual, rather than the public good. Ever more costly, sophisticated and speculative technological approaches are being directed to ever less frequent or tractable diseases (such as those that plague old age), rather than the age-old plagues that affect vast numbers of people in poor countries, and that require low-tech solutions.

Appropriateness and achievability. Not all diseases can be cured, and individualised medicine may not be feasible. The enormous benefits anticipated by Wilmut[107] may not be realised[108], while there may be simpler ways of achieving the same ends. Gage[109] describes work to mobilise neural stem cells following strokes, but emphasises that the brain is best supported when people eat, rest and exercise well.

Desirability. Mombaerts[110] suggests that autologous ESCs could be used when our aging body is wearing out due to cell loss. Holm[111] speaks of rejuvenating therapies leading to increased lifespan. Longevity might be a goal in a society where death is the unmentionable word, but propping up failing organs in aging bodies is

---

104. Rhind, 'Human Cloning: Can It Be Made Safe?', *op cit.*
105. McLaren, 'Ethical and Social Considerations of Stem Cell Research', *op cit.*
106. Shannon, 'Human Embryonic Stem Cell Therapy', *op cit.*
107. Wilmut, 'The Moral Imperative for Human Cloning', *op cit.*
108. McLaren, 'Ethical and Social Considerations of Stem Cell Research', *op cit.*
109. FH Gage, 'Brain, Repair Yourself', *Scientific American* (2003): 46–52.
110. Mombaerts, 'Therapeutic Cloning in the Mouse', *op cit.*
111. Holm, 'Going to the Roots of the Stem Cell Controversy', *op cit.*

not an inspiring goal. We need to be reminded, as Turner[112] has done, that biotechnology 'has all the social power of a belief system or a surrogate religion'. This is instantiated when we encounter 'technoevangelists' who proclaim that 'somatic cell nuclear transfer, stem cell research and regenerative medicine . . . will enable researchers to slow or reverse aging processes and permit humans to live prolonged lives'. Biotech fantasies offer 'the prospect of a this-worldly form of life extension.' And their effects on credulous and fearful individuals are far from benign.

Priority. The current heavy preoccupation with 'genethics' is leading to the neglect of other important ethical, legal, and social factors that affect human health and wellbeing. Turner[113] is concerned that an overemphasis on 'genethics' to the exclusion of other pressing considerations is promoting misallocation of research money, disregard of social issues (malnutrition, poverty, AIDS), and sequestration of research and teaching expertise.

An anonymous researcher has stated: 'I find it astonishing that people complain bitterly about the perceived threat of genetics to human dignity when they see grotesque insults to human dignity all around them and they do nothing about it'.[114] While the Christian must address the ethics of therapeutic cloning with humility, openness and a lack of dogmatism, there are ethical issues for which appropriate responses are patently obvious. Poverty affecting children's development, health and education has everything to do with dignity (a concept so frequently utilised in the context of the human embryo). C Everett Koop[115] agonised over the tolerance shown towards the tobacco industry, asking 'Where is the outrage?' It remains true that there are many pressing issues for which decisive, passionate, and sacrificial Christian action is required to demonstrate the reality of their concern for human dignity. Only by so doing will they earn the right to be heard on abstruse bioethical issues.

112. L Turner, 'Biotechnology as Religion', *Nature Biotechnology* 22 (2004): 659–660.
113. L Turner, 'The Tyranny of "Genethics"'. *Nature Biotechnology* 21 (2003): 1282.
114. D Butler and M Wadman, 'Calls for Cloning Ban sell Science Short', *Nature* 386 (1997): 8–9.
115. CE Koop, 'The Tobacco Scandal: Where is the Outrage?', *Tobacco Control* 7 (1998): 393–396.

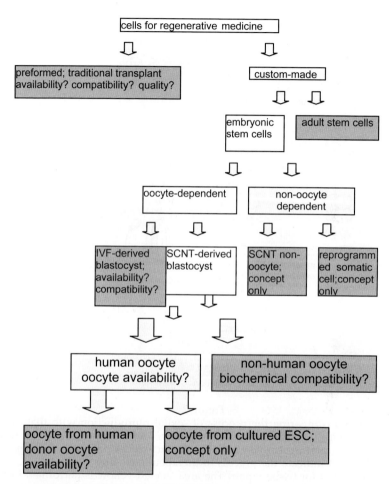

Figure 1.
Flow diagram illustrating various possible strategies for obtaining cells for tissue replacement and regeneration.

Shaded boxes represent current or conceivable sources of tissue for regenerative medicine. Only the 'traditional transplant' is currently available as a therapeutic procedure. Only SCNT-derived cells would be generated by therapeutic cloning.

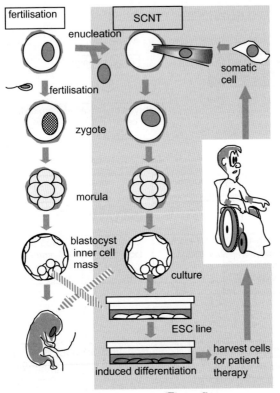

Figure 2:
A diagram comparing the process of sexual reproduction with that of cloning, both reproductive and therapeutic. The sequence of events on the left indicates the early events in reproductive development; the steps on the right indicate the process of therapeutic cloning by which ESCs are generated for tissue repair. The area shaded yellow is performed in culture.

The cross-hatched arrows indicate the possibilities that a reproductively-derived blastocyst could be used as a source of (allogeneic) cells for therapy; and a blastocyst arising from a cloned adult cell could be implanted in a uterus to generate a baby (the process of 'reproductive cloning', a procedure that is not currently feasible in humans, and that is universally regarded as ethically wrong).

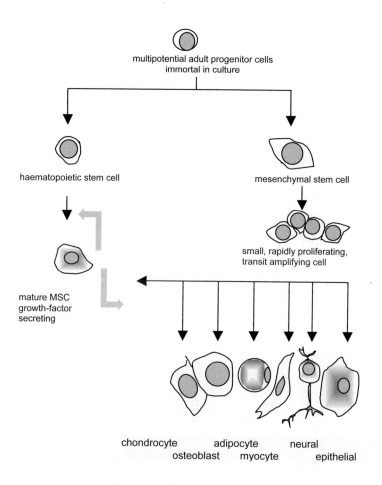

Figure 3.
The potential for using bone-marrow derived MSCs to generate a range of specialised cell types *in vitro*. Not all authors are careful to differentiate between the haematopoietic and mesenchymal stem cell populations from marrow.

The diagram is modified from Prockop *et al* 2003.

Table 1

Potency and location of stem cells

stem cell potency	cell types
totipotent	fertilised egg
	blastomere, a near descendent of a fertilized egg cell produced by SCNT* (?)
pluripotent	embryonic stem cell of blastocyst inner cell mass arising from fertilisation or SCNT
	fetal germ cell
multipotent	bone marrow haematopoietic;
	bone marrow mesenchymal;
	neural and others

* SCNT, somatic cell nuclear transfer
Adapted from Cogle *et al* 2003.

Table 2

Pluripotent ES cells derived by nuclear transfer (mouse and human*)

donor cell	efficiency, % ESC lines / fusion	mature cell types generated		reference
		in vitro	*in vivo*	
cumulus cell	0.11	muscle, neuronal	all germ layers, cells in many organs	Munsie et al 2000
cumulus, tail tip cells	3.4	glial, neuronal	all organs, gametes	Wakayama et al 2001 Barberi et al 2003
lymphocyte	0.21	not done	viable mice	Hochedlinger and Jaenisch 2002
tail tip	0.48	blood stem cell	fertile mice	Rideout et al 200
neuron	0.88	not done	fertile mice	Eggan et al 2004
cumulus cell*	0.63–0.96	3 germ layers	3 germ layers teratomas in mice	Hwang et al 2004

The 'donor cells' are those used to provide a nucleus for SCNT.
Efficiencies represent the percentage of SCNT oocytes that gave rise to an ESC line.
The 'mature cell types' represent the specialized types of cells that are derived from ESCs, either in culture or in the body.

38

Table 3

The epigenetic barrier to development

structure	chromosome source	development potential	limitation to development
hydatidiform mole (placental tissue)	paternal	none	epigenetic*
ovarian teratoma (many tissues)	maternal	none	epigenetic
parthenogenetic embryo	maternal	none	epigenetic**
SCNT embryo	somatic cell	v.low / none	epigenetic?
fertilised embryo (80% of embryos)	biparental	none	genetic?
fertilized embryo (20% of embryos)	biparental	high	none

* only the 'complete' hydatidiform mole arises from two haploid (23,X) sperm nuclei
** except where genetic modifications inactivate epigenetic mechanisms, Kono et al 2004.

Table 4

Possible distinction of blastocysts depending on networks of relationships

somatic cell-derived blastocyst	fertilization-derived blastocyst
generated by technically contrived method	generated by divinely ordained process of sexual fusion
outcome of an impersonal manipulation	expression of a personal relationship
artifact of laboratory skill	embodiment of parental love
product for therapeutic (medical) purpose	a human being with relational purpose
strictly *in vitro* environment	strictly *in utero* environment
no maternal environment	maternal environment (blood supply, hormones)
extension of tissues of an existing person	a new creation from the union of two people
extrinsic to human relationality, sociality, sexuality	intrinsic to human relationality, sociality, sexuality
outside the relational context of human being	shares in our status as human being
legitimate source of cells to treat the donor	requires diligent protection as human being

Table 5

Basic research required for adult stem cell use

Stem cell biology	*scientific unknown*
nature of stem cells	BM stem cells are likely to be a heterogeneous population
	identity of useful markers for stem cell populations
	the sources and location of stem cells in tissues
administration	the number of stem cells needed for engraftment
	the routes of administration
	the appropriate time of implantation (relative to early inflammation and later fibrogenesis);
homing	the mechanisms that guide cell homing
	the nature of chemoattractants that recruit stem cells to sites of damage
	whether cell homing *in vivo* is perturbed by prior cell culture
engraftment	the ability of stem cells to reconstitute an ischaemic site populated with inflammatory cells
	the role of cell-cell contact in directing stem cell lineage selection and differentiation;
	the nature and adequacy of tissue cues for inducing differentiation of stem cells;
	the role of stem cell fusion with resident cells
	the ability to induce and co-ordinate neovascularisation

Interface 7/2 (October 2004)

Stem Cell Research:
Theological and Contextual Considerations

Elizabeth Hepburn IBVM
Canberra

1.Introduction

The topic of stem cell research raises two critical questions which are quite different in character. However, both bear on the issue of how we see ourselves as humans and how we think of our relationships with others.

The first question is whether we should be pursuing research on stem cells, research which promises so much to some afflicted with terrible diseases, when so many of those already living members of the human community go to bed hungry each night, or worse.

The second question is at first sight not related but I will argue says just as much about how we regard ourselves and those around us. It is the question of the status of the embryo and what our obligations are to embryos.

2. A case in point

The questions of the status of the embryo were raised very eloquently in a cartoon published in the Melbourne *Age* newspaper in 1984[1] when the issue of what should be done with the Rios twins was before the court. In this cartoon Nicholson depicted a group of men-medicos, legal eagles, clergymen, academics-standing around a test tube which bears a tag saying 'orphan embryos' and one of the men is saying, 'We must find a solution to this problem'. Not a single person depicted is capable of being a mother. It reminds one of Solomon's decision about the baby brought before him (1 Kings 3:16-28); he thought that the person who would decide in the best interests of the infant was the mother.

---

1.   Nicholson, *Age*, 14 June 1984.

The 'problem' was what should be done with the embryos of an Argentinian couple called Rios, and left behind in a freezer in Melbourne. Mrs Rios had become pregnant through IVF conducted in a Melbourne clinic and returned to Argentina to await the birth of her babe. Tragically, the couple were killed in a plane crash. The issue before the court was how the very considerable Rios estate should be divided.

If it could be established that the embryos were the children of the Rios couple they may be the rightful inheritors of a fortune; if that were not the case, then the embryos would constitute part of the estate to be divided. The outcome depended on whether the embryos are regarded as persons and subjects, or seen as mere cells and property or objects.

Nicholson, though, saw more problems than the dilemma over the status of the embryos. In the other half of his cartoon he drew a number of vaguely Asiatic figures, poorly clad and standing beneath a sign which said 'Third World'. He posed the question, do we have the right to invest in technology to reproduce ourselves while there are so many members of the human community condemned to starvation?

It seems to me that while the Rios predicament raised countless questions these two are really central to the way in which we think about technology and ourselves as human beings.

3. The status of the embryo and stem cell research

There are basically three ways of thinking about personhood. The first is to take the development of the person as continuous from the point of conception. The second is to regard personal life as beginning at birth, when the child is recognised in most jurisdictions as a person. The third is to restrict the notion of personhood to those who demonstrate they possess consciousness and mental capacity.

The Catholic tradition in moral theology sees the interpolation of various markers of development as arbitrary and claims that the human individual is developing in a unique way, from conception; in short; 'It would never be made human if it were not human already.'[2]

The Vatican stops short of calling the embryo a person but says that since it is impossible to know what the status is, we should give it the

2.   Sacred Congregation for the Doctrine of the Faith, *Declaration on Abortion* (Homebush: St Paul's, 1974).

benefit of the doubt and treat it as if it were a person. Donum Vitae says: 'The human being must be respected—as a person—from the very first instance of his existence'. And later 'in the zygote[3] resulting from fertilization the biological identity of a new human individual is already constituted'.[4]

The same insistence on the protection of the child is voiced in the United Nations Declaration on the Rights of the Child. In the preamble it states; 'The child, by reason of his physical and mental infirmity, needs special safeguards and care, including appropriate legal protection, before as well as after birth'.[5]

In support of this premise there was a case in Queensland in which damage to an unborn child by physical attack, kicking, was deemed violence not only to the mother carrying the child, but also to the child.[6] This seems to imply rights on the part of both the child and the mother.

The political difficulty in conferring rights on the foetus is that it counters the view that a woman has a right to determine her own reproductive future. This view holds that a woman has no obligation to support the life within her while it is dependent on her for nutrition and hydration; thus birth becomes the point at which the child may have rights. The claim on behalf of the child after birth for injuries sustained before birth muddies the waters considerably.

The whole question becomes more complex with advances in foetal surgery, who is the patient and whose interests do we proceed to champion? While I was a student in the United States in 1993 my class was confronted by an engaging young woman who introduced herself as a fetologist. She said that she was committed to acting in the best interests of her patient, the foetus. No sooner had she finished than she was joined at the lectern by an equally eloquent young man, who said he was an obstetrician and committed to serving the best interests of the woman. Immediately the stage was set for conflict in a relationship

---

3.   'Zygote' here is understood as a cell in which the nuclei of two gamete cells have fused.

4.   Sacred Congregation for the Doctrine of the Faith, *Donum Vitae* (Homebush: St Paul's, 1987) Section I:1,19, 21, 22.

5.   United Nations, *Declaration on the Rights of the Child* (United Nations, 1959).

6.   L Edmiston, 'Death Renews Debate over Unborn', *The Courier-Mail* (Saturday 27 September 2003).

which was previously thought to be about the most intimate human connection possible.

Reviewing just a couple of legal issues shows that the law is far from clear on the matter and we have some unease with what we believe about the child before birth

We are faced with the fact that a foetus may undergo surgery and sue for damages after birth and laws which do not recognise it as a legal entity until after birth. The Queensland Parliament debated this at length with suggestions that the time at which rights pertained be specified, but ended with no such specification.

4. Stem cells and cloning

Those who believe that the child has human rights conferred at birth or later are able to say that we ought be free to treat the foetus as we will, as a source of tissues, as isolated cells and stem cells. Certainly, the hopes of finding radically new ways of treating disease seem wonderful. But are we right to conceive a child, principally to provide cells for a sick sibling or to replace a sibling? Is this an act which commodifies humans in a way which makes slavery look humane?

Reports of work in Korea raise a number of related problems. It seems that there has been some success in cloning human embryos. Hwang[7] reports having grown embryonic stem cells for therapeutic use by replacing the haploid nucleus of an ovum with the diploid nucleus from another part of the woman's body. Therapeutic cloning of this sort and reproductive cloning are currently banned in Australia; the ban is to be reviewed in two years' time.

The moral question is whether it is right to raise these embryos at all. The embryos are exactly like the person from whom the nuclear material is obtained, and live only to supply the stem cells which will be totipotent. The removal of the embryonic stem cells is generally fatal to the embryo. Thus the embryo is treated as a means to an end.

A secondary question which arises is how we are going to keep therapeutic applications of cloning separate from reproductive cloning. It is true that reproductive cloning at least assures the embryo of life, but to what end? The evidence of Dolly and subsequent animal clones has been that they inherit the biological mother's age and so the diseases of aging afflict the offspring. The conflation of the two

7.   WS Hwang, *Science*, reported in *The Sydney Morning Herald* (Friday 13 February 2004), 3.

purposes of cloning shows that it is important to know how we think of the embryo.

The cloning of embryos for therapeutic purposes requires its proponents to argue that there is no person present to be considered. The cloning of embryos for reproductive purposes, however, demands that those who desire to create a child this way invest the being with personality; the last thing they want to be accused of is using technology in a perverted way. Critics of this obsession to immortalise oneself claim that the child will be subject to all sorts of strange desires and expectations.

What appears to happen once we abandon the notion of attributing the rights of a human being to the embryo is that we must choose a time at which we say that 'rights' must now begin to be observed. There are several candidates: the appearance of the so-called 'primitive streak', usually about fifteen days after fertilisation; the time up until which abortion may be legally performed in some countries, which varies between twelve and twenty-eight weeks from conception; the point of viability, ie at which the foetus if born would be capable of sustaining life, usually taken to be twenty-four weeks; and the point of birth. In addition, there is the possibility of attaching significance to attributes of the person and making 'personhood' contingent upon the possession of these. Thus several classes of 'non-persons' become possibilities, for instance the permanently unconscious, which space does not permit me to explore here.

Instantly, problems can be seen with each of these important marker events. It seems to me they all arise from the fact that development is not a staged process but a continuous one. Practical difficulties arise because the staging itself is imprecise, the actual time of conception is not known, except in the case of IVF, and the estimates of entry into stages is always going to be an average figure. Some embryos and foetuses will develop quickly and some slowly, and to attach significance to a particular event or date can be misleading.

Clearly, the point of birth is a choice which few would dispute, but even there we have disagreement. If the vital thing about being a person is seen in terms of capabilities then it could be argued that depriving the newborn of life is not a crime. Singer[8] has argued just

---

8.   Peter Singer & Helga Kuhse, 'Resolving Arguments about the Sanctity of Life: A Reply to Long', *Journal of Medical Ethics* 14 (1985): 198–199.

this way, claiming that newborns do not have hopes or plans for the future and hence have no interest in their own future. Thus the killing of infants does not deprive them of anything they value. Indeed, I heard Peter say in answer to a question that he thought the development of this capacity occurred at about three years of age.

Most importantly, the basis of the argument for using human embryonic stem cells in a way which is fatal to the embryo is justified on the grounds that the embryo does not have the rights of a person. As Soren Holm[9] points out, the strict consequentialist line does not take the personhood argument very seriously at all. Singer's preference for seeing the development of the capacity to make choices as a threshold serves to shift the time at which personhood is identifiable. This puts him on a continuum with those who Holm calls 'gradualists', who actually give the embryo moral status and see this as something which becomes more valuable with maturity.

The real stumbling-block with the view that the embryo ought be treated with the respect due a person is that it would commit proponents to taking an anti-abortion stance, and for many this would be uncomfortable. We are, in liberal, Western-style democracies, guilty of doing a double-think on this question. If the foetus is worthy of protection because it has potential for extra-corporeal life then surely the embryo is also a person, because it is only a matter of extending the capabilities of the neo-natal intensive care unit. This is at least as possible as the hoped-for benefits of stem cell therapy.

Finally, if the embryo has the status of a person then the Rios twins would be the rightful inheritors of the Rios estate, and a Tasmanian Supreme Court ruled this way in 1996.[10] In short, our thinking about these issues is far from clear and the status of the human embryo remains a matter of debate.

5. The social justice of stem cell research

Advocates of human stem cell research believe that the ability of the cells to develop into cells as directed mean that many diseases could be cured by this technique. They admit that it is probably a long way off.

Peter Singer, *Rethinking Life and Death* (Melbourne: The Text Publishing Company, 1994).

9.   Soren Holm, 'The Ethical Case against Stem Cell Research', *Cambridge Quarterly of Healthcare Ethics*, (2003): 372–383.

10.   *Re Estate of K A* (Tas Supreme Court, Slicer J, April 1996) 16/1996.

However, the dream is to be able to replace the cells and organs lost through disease or accident. The ability to clone cells provides the opportunity to overcome rejection by minimising the differences between donor and recipient.

The people who would benefit are those who could afford to meet the costs of this new technology and they are comparatively few in number. So would this be a just way in which to spend our 'health' dollars? Would we be better off attending to the disease which costs more people their lives than any other, malaria? We already know how to make environments mosquito-free, but lack the political will to do so. Clean water supplies which are not infested with mosquitoes would render other water-born infections things of the past.

Further, if communities were not ravaged by malaria, dysentery, tuberculosis and so on the economic life of the developing world would be greatly enhanced. Healthy communities deliver so many human, social goods which are denied societies burdened with disease. The educational aspirations of the children would grow if they were not too sick to attend, and that in turn would feed into a vigorous economy.

In an interesting collection of essays written in honour of Enda McDonough, two theologians, Gabriel Daly[11] and Nicholas Lash,[12] decry the current tendency of church leaders to shun engagement with the world and to prefer to talk in language which only the initiated understand. Both of them talk of a need to retrieve a holistic sense of what it is to be human and to reject the dualism of Descartes.

Talking about the links between mysticism and contemporary ways of seeing the world, Daly recalls the claims of Von Hugel that we need philosophy, religion and science to understand the world. Further, religion properly understood requires the interplay of three components also, these being the institutional, the intellectual and the mystical. The mystical he saw as the mark of maturity and the appropriate corrective for the institutional with its emphasis on authority and the intellectual with its emphasis on the rational. The correction he describes is to interpolate experience with the other two commitments. He says: 'It brings the intuitive, emotional, experiential,

---

11. Gabriel Daly, 'Mysticism and Modernism', in *Between Politics and Poetry*, edited by L Hogan & B FitzGerald (Dublin: The Columba Press, 2003), 16–31.

12. Nicholas Lash, 'Conversation in Context', in *Between Politics and Poetry*, edited by L Hogan & B FitzGerald (Dublin: The Columba Press, 2003), 51–66.

and volitional to complement and correct the institutional and intellectual both of which tend to resist the mystical'.[13]

It seems to me that this is what is missing from discussions about the rights and wrongs of how we deal with the embryo and where that fits with our thinking about humanity at large. The church has been forceful in saying what we ought and ought not do to embryos but seems relatively silent on our responsibilities to distribute the goods the earth produces on a fair and equitable basis. The disconnection between these two aspects of our human life together seems odd until we see what has happened in theology. Our thinking has become detached from experience, and the mystical is viewed with suspicion. It seems that intuition and emotion have no place in our moral evaluation of what we ought do.

Nicholas Lash blames Descartes and Galileo for driving the division between us and the world in which we live. Our prizing of objectivity means that the 'local' and the 'global' concerns which are highlighted in Nicholson's cartoon, as what to do with the embryo and what that means for our treatment of world starvation, are never allowed each to cast light on the other. He thinks that when we scrutinise this habit of mind we are bound to see the futility it brings. Lash puts it this way: 'This separation of consciousness from nature, of speech and thought from what we speak and think about, sustained the illusion that we can speak the truth from nowhere in particular, that "reason" springs from no particular soil, knows no particular place or time'.[14]

It is something of this dialogue with reality which I would like to see brought to bear on the question of justice and the uses of technology. Unless, like Nicholson, we begin to seriously ask the hard questions about the distribution of resources by the rich in the face of blinding poverty of our fellow human beings out of a recognition that my self-concern is robbing them of the necessities of life, there is little point in arguing about when life begins.

6. Conclusion

I have tried to explain why I see the question of the moral status of the embryo and the pursuit of stem cell research as related, as both having something to say about humanity. For I think that only by divorcing

---

13.   Daly, 'Mysticism and Modernism', *op cit*, 26.

14.   Lash, 'Conversation in Context', *op cit*, 57.

ourselves from reality can we think that they are entirely separate. If the embryo is worthy of consideration, and I believe it is, then questions of justice and the necessity of working to save the lives of those who already share the earth with us cannot be ignored. For in the words of a man who was able to marry the disciplines of philosophy, religion and science: 'To understand the world knowledge is not enough. You must live it, breathe it and drink the vital heat of existence in the heart of reality' (Teilhard de Chardin SJ).

Until We Have Faces: Viewing Stem Cell Research and Other Biomedical Technologies in an Eschatological Frame

Ian Barns
Perth

1. Introduction

Much of the intense ethical debate surrounding stem cell research has been centred on the issue of their primary source: unused embryos left over from IVF procedures. The question of whether it is ethical to harvest stem cells from human embryos (either from IVF procedures or produced specifically for research purposes), and in the process destroying them, has been the focus of several major inquiries in various countries and has led to carefully crafted guidelines which have allowed the use of embryonic stem cells (ESC), though under restricted conditions. From the point of view of the major opponents such use is tantamount to the destruction of human beings.[1] The counter view is that such unwanted embryos would in the fullness of time be discarded anyway and that it is ethically appropriate that they be used for good purposes in the treatment of degenerative diseases such as Parkinson's and Alzheimer's.

This particular debate thus expresses in a new context the long-standing controversy over the status of the human embryo that has been central to abortion politics and to the regulation of embryo research. At the same time, the advent of stem cell research increases the complexity of the issue, for example in the procedure of so-called therapeutic cloning (SCNT, somatic cell nuclear transfer), which involves the creation of an embryo from the processes of transferring the nucleus from a somatic cell into an enucleated egg cell.

When framed in these terms, the ethical problem of stem cell research is considered to be resolvable if and when the alternative

---

1.   Robert P George, 'The Ethics of Embryonic Stem Cell Research and Human Cloning', *Family Research Council Newsletter*, Issue 87 (http://www.frc.org/get.cfm?i=PD02D5 posted June 9, 2004).

source of adult stem cells becomes an effective substitute for ESCs. Whilst not always regarded as flexible as ESCs in their range of application, the use of adult stem cells nonetheless avoids the problem of destroying embryos. In the light of this, many conservative opponents fully approve of the positive potential of (adult) stem cell research and application. Their ethical reservations are not to do with stem cell research as such.

However, this particular framing of the ethics of stem cell research is too narrow and obscures the broader and more profound ethical challenges associated with emerging biomedical technologies of which stem cell research is a part.[2] This array of technologies opens up longer term possibilities of deeper level biomedical intervention, dealing with degenerative diseases and creating new possibilities for the biomedical enhancement of human bodies, brains and behaviour. Although stem cell research represents just one particular develop-ment, it does, along with the completion of the human genome project and human cloning, symbolise the remarkable increase in the capacity to understand and modify many of the complex processes that make up the human organism.

When seen in this broader context, stem cell research needs to be debated, not just in terms of the moral status of embryos, but in terms of the larger meanings and moral trajectory of biomedicine as a whole.

Of course, there is now a well-established literature of bioethical reflection on the familiar gamut of biomedical developments, especially those associated with reproductive technologies, gene therapy and the use of powerful drug therapies. What is striking, though, about much of the mainstream debate is that such technologies are assumed to be no more than powerful tools that can be carefully evaluated in terms of an institutionalised framework of ethical deliberation and administrative regulation.[3] Such discussion deploys

---

2.   See Audrey Chapman, *Unprecedented Choices: Religious Ethics at the Frontiers of Genetic Science* (Minneapolis, MI, Fortress Press, 1999).

3.   In their report, *Stem Cell Research and Applications Monitoring the Frontiers of Biomedical Research,* Produced by the American Association for the Advancement of Science and Institute for Civil Society, Nov 1999, Audrey Chapman, Mark Frankel and Michele Garfinkel comment: 'Although some adjustments in the current system of oversight are necessary, no new regulatory mechanisms are needed at the present time to ensure responsible social and professional control of such research in the United States. A system that has, over

the familiar language of ethical principles in the instrumental use of technology: avoiding harm, protecting rights, ensuring equality of access, and so on.

However, the rapidly developing biomedical technologies, including those which will make use of stem cells, pose ethical challenges that modernist bioethics cannot adequately address. The ethical significance of such technologies goes beyond questions of how they are used. More profoundly they increase the possibilities of altering the very nature and conditions of human existence itself (by increasing lifespan, enhancing physical performance, augmenting anatomical and other features and modifying brain function, including memory enhancement, emotional states, and so forth). As Fukuyama has argued, they open up the possibility of a 'posthuman future'.[4] In the light of this, the central ethical questions are not just those of ensuring the use of technologies in fair and non-harmful ways, but of whether and in what ways our very 'humanness' will be modified in the process. In turn this raises the deep and long-standing question of just what it is that makes us 'human' anyway.

2. Technologising human beings

The new biotechnologies promise/ threaten to alter our humanness in a number of ways. The most obvious level is that of the specific technological developments which promise to increase the degree of quality control of human reproduction, development and physical and mental performance: embryonic selection, germ line modification, gene therapy, enhancement technologies, increasing lifespan, cybernetic extensions, and so on.[5] As the President's Bioethics Council observed,

---

time, protected the public health and safety while simultaneously providing a setting that is congenial to the advancement of science has much to offer'.

4. Francis Fukuyama, *Our Posthuman Future: Consequences of the Biotechnology Revolution* (New York, Farrar, Straus and Giroux, 2002).

5. Eric Parens (ed), *Enhancing Human Traits: Ethical and Social Implications*, Washington (Georgetown: Georgetown University Press, 1998); Damien Broderick, *The Last Mortal Generation: How Science Will Alter Our Lives in the 21st Century* (Sydney: New Holland Publishers, 1999); Brian Appleyard, *Brave New Worlds: Genetics and the Human Experience* (London: HarperCollins 1999).

it is likely that the techniques will go 'beyond therapy' to enable quite significant enhancements, the creation of posthuman people.[6]

However, these emerging techniques are not the only, or even the most important, changes that bring our humanness into question. There are a number of contextual factors which lie behind and shape the specific biotechnological innovations which are equally as if not more important in technologising (or geneticising or medicalising) the human condition. The first is the array of institutionalised biomedical practices operating at the level of healthcare, particularly in hospitals, and clinics. The patterns of institutionalised care and treatment, involving increasingly sophisticated biomedical treatment, establish or reinforce certain conceptions of the human body and the human person which subtly undermine the coherence and integrity of the human agent.[7] They consolidate practices of the human body which result in, not only the fragmentation of the body, but a way of viewing and experiencing ourselves as complex machines whose performance can be modified through various medical interventions and monitoring.[8]

The second is the broader economic, political and cultural context of capitalist late modernity. As many commentators have noted, the shifts in political economy in recent decades, particularly those associated with emerging ICTs and biotechnologies, have facilitated, not only the networks of a global economy, but also a pervasive commodification and individualisation of human life and relationships within a market society.[9] The economic opportunities for increased profit through the creation of new products and services for new

6.   Leon Kass *et al*, *Beyond Therapy: Biotechnology and the Pursuit of Happiness. A Report of the President's Council on Bioethics* (Washington, DC, 2003).

7.   Arthur Frank *The Wounded Storyteller: Body, Illness and Ethics* (Chicago: University of Chicago Press, 1995).

8.   See Doug White, 'Divide and Multiply: Culture and Politics in the New Medical Order', in *Troubled Bodies: Critical Perspectives on Postmodernism, Medical Ethics and the Body*, edited by Paul Komesaroff (Melbourne: Melbourne University Press, 1995).

9.   Albert Borgmann *Crossing the Post-modern Divide* (Chicago: University of Chicago Press, 1992); Anthony Giddens, *Modernity and Self Identity: Self and Society in the Late Modern Age* (Stanford: Stanford University Press, 1991); Ken Gergen *The Saturated Self: Dilemmas of Identity in Contemporary Life* (New York: Basic Books, 1990).

markets, especially in the area of pharmaceutical drugs and health products, have been the catalyst for changes in the core political institutions of late modern societies, such that few areas of life are untouched by an increasingly ruthless market logic. To be sure there has been a revival of notions of civil society, social capital, civic governance and the like, but these are framed within, and thus conditioned by, the moral horizon of consumer markets.[10]

Thirdly, the accounts of human evolutionary development that undergird contemporary explanations of human behaviour and consciousness also subtly and profoundly change our sense of what it is to be human. Of course the Darwinian view of the world has been with us for some time. However, in recent times it is being brought more directly into the interpretive understanding of human experience, particularly in areas such as sociobiology, evolutionary psychology and genetics.[11] A Darwinian account of human origins percolates through popular accounts of matters of human propensity to violence, gender strategies, and so forth. We thus learn to see ourselves as ultimately arbitrary constructions whose genetic blueprint and phenotypic expression are the outcome of processes of selection within ancient environments. We, the resultant organisms, are far from perfectly formed. Indeed, we are jerry-built adaptations, only opportunistically adapted to fit the demands of past environments, and perhaps even less hardwired for the ecologies of late industrial societies.

The consequence of these techno-scientific and cultural developments is a profound shift in the way we understand not just the capacities of human beings, but our ontology as well. We come to see ourselves as complex, imperfectly designed biological machines whose capacities are the result of the slow selective processes of evolutionary change operating on the hidden potential of complex material systems. Within this techno-scientific explanatory approach, there seems little need for some additional soul-like substance to account for human cognitive, emotional, social and even spiritual experience. All of these higher functions can be understood as the emergent products of

---

10. Carl Elliott, 'The Pursuit of Happiness', *Atlantic Monthly* online August 2003, http://www.theatlantic.com/unbound/interviews/int2003-08-05.htm.

11. For example, see Dean Hamer and Peter Copeland, *Living with Our Genes: Why They Matter More Than You Think* (London: Pan Books, 2000).

complex genetic, biochemical and neurological processes operating within a world of symbolically mediated social interaction.

Erik Davis describes this in terms of our becoming 'spiritual cyborgs': an outcome which reflects the demise of the Cartesian project which attempted to preserve the specialness of humans within a material world understood primarily in terms of purposeless mechanism.[12] Of course Davis is using the term 'cyborgs' metaphorically, rather than as a literal description of a fusion of human bodies with machines. We have become conceptually and spiritually cyborgs insofar as we come to understand ourselves increasingly as complex bio-cybernetic systems open in principle to continuous technological remodelling.[13]

3. Debating our posthuman future

Over the past few years a lively debate has developed about the desirability or otherwise of moving towards a posthuman future, ranging from the strident confidence of techno-utopians through to the dystopian concerns of the so-called bio-luddites or bio-conservatives. It is beyond the scope of this discussion to review this debate in any details. Rather I want to briefly outline what I consider to be the four main responses to the posthuman(ist) implications of emerging human biotechnologies. In doing so I am primarily interested in how these responses deal with the distinctiveness of moral experience and personal identity of human existence in the post-Cartesian context of a radical techno-scientific reconstruction of humans being.[14]

---

12.   Erik Davis 'The Spiritual Cyborgs', in *TechGnosis: Myth, Magic and Mysticism in an Age of Information* (New York: Harmony Books, 1998); see also Erik Davis, 'Synthetic Mediations: Cogito in the Matrix' in *Prefiguring Cyberculture: An Intellectual History*, edited by Darren Tofts, Annemarie Jonson and Alession Cavallaro (Cambridge: MIT Press, 2002) for a discussion of the continuing influence of Cartesian dualism in cyberculture discourse.

13.   See also Katherine Hayles, *How We Became Posthuman: Virtual Bodies in Cybernetics, Literature, and Informatics* (Chicago: University of Chicago Press, 1999).

14.   This taxonomy is largely adapted from that used by Nicholas Smith in his account of different hermeneutical responses to the crisis of human ontology resulting from the project of 'enlightenment fundamentalism'. See Nicholas Smith *Strong Hermeneutics: Contingency and Moral Identity* (London: Routledge, 1997).

3.1 The techno-optimists

Recent developments in the key fields of genetics, robotics and nanotechnology have prompted a growing number of scientists and others to confidently proclaim a bright future for the radical enhancement of the human condition through technology. In the field of human genetics this includes most prominently scientists such as Gregory Stock and Lee Silver.[15] Both consider that the adoption of genetic technologies to modify our descendents are inevitable and desirable. Stock is a supporter of germ-line engineering. Silver accepts that in a market society, there will be an inevitable adoption of improvement technologies leading to a gradual bifurcation of an existing human species into the 'Gen-rich' and the 'naturals', a division that will ultimately result in two separate species.

Surrounding the comparatively measured views of the scientists is a remarkable array of techno-utopians,[16] such as the Extropians whose sunny confidence can be illustrated by the 'letter to nature' written by their leader Max More:

> Truly we are grateful for what you have made us. No doubt you did the best you could. However with all due respect, we must say that you have in many ways done a poor job with the human constitution. You have made us vulnerable to disease and damage. You

---

15. Gregory Stock, *Redesigning Humans: Choosing our Children's Genes* (London: Profile Books, 2002); Lee Silver, *Remaking Eden: Cloning, Genetic Engineering and the Future of Humankind?* (London: Phoenix Books, 1999).

16. Reporting on a Transhumanist Vision 2003 conference, Carl Elliott observed, 'So the question recurs: Should we be paying attention? I think we should. As far over the edge as the transhumanists often appear, they represent a number of ideological strands evident throughout American society. One is a brand of individualistic, libertarian ideology often associated with Silicon Valley. A second is independent, quasi-religious thinking of the sort that sometimes leads to new religious communities, such as the Mormons, but that more often is disguised as disdain toward organized religion. A third is idealistic faith in the power of technology to make the world a better place. To look at the transhumanist movement and its self-identified enemies is to glimpse some of the ideological battle grounds where the debate over new enhancement technologies will be conducted.' Carl Elliott, Humanity 2.0' *Wilson Quarterly Autumn* 2003 (http://wwics.si.edu/index.cfm?fuseaction=wq.essay&essay_id=69342).

compel us to age and die—just as we're beginning to
attain wisdom. And you forgot to give us the
operating manual for ourselves! What you have made
is glorious, yet deeply flawed . . . We have decided
that it is time to amend the human constitution . . . We
do not do this lightly, carelessly or disrespectfully,
but cautiously, intelligently and in pursuit of
excellence . . . Over the coming decades we will
pursue a series of changes to our own constitution . . .
We will no longer tolerate the tyranny of aging and
death . . . We will expand our perceptual range . . .
Improve on our neural organization and capacity . . .
reshape our motivational patterns and emotional
responses . . . take charge over genetic programming
and achieve mastery over our biological and
neurological processes.[17]

What is perhaps most remarkable about this new generation of
techno-utopians is their supreme confidence in the unalloyed
progressive benefits of emerging technologies. They contemptuously
dismiss the bio-conservatives or bio-luddites such as Leon Kass. There
is little evidence of concern for the dystopian possibilities of the
application of such technologies, either in terms of the political
consequences[18] or the implications for the humanist tradition that has
hitherto sustained the ethic of human rights.

Despite their enthusiastic advocacy for the rapid technologising of
human beings, the techno-optimists continue to tacitly assume the
autonomy of the (Cartesian) rational self, though not as a moral agent
committed to the moral dignity of all human persons, but to the further
empowerment of an enhanced elite. It is no coincidence that their
techno-utopian ideology fits so well with the competitive freedom of a
free market society.

---

17.   Max More, 'Letter to Mother Nature', (August 1999)
      (http://www.maxmore.com/mother.htm).

18.   Cf Bill Joy's now famous essay expressing deep concern about the dangers arising
      from the new technologies: 'Why the Future Doesn't Need Us', *Wired Magazine*
      8.04, (April 2000).

3.2 Postmodern posthumanism

A second, very different perspective is that of a range of postmodernist interpreters of our posthuman or 'cyborg' condition. For such writers, the cyborg becomes the central metaphor for the pervasive technologising of human practice, discourse and ontology. Postmodern theorists have become particularly interested in the discourses and practices (as much as the specific techniques) of late modern technology, particularly those of IT and biotechnology, because of their contribution to destabilising the essentialised self of Western humanism. The rupturing and fragmentation of the humanist (masculinist) self and the erosion of the boundaries between the self and the other, including machines and the non-human world has, in their view, created new emancipatory possibilities for new kinds of human being and community. In this context, as Annemarie Jonson and Darren Tofts put it:

> The figure of the cyborg has emerged as a kind of totem for this emerging state of otherness, a state that presages the ascendency of a dramatic new phylum—the posthuman. The posthuman is a category or classification of life that goes beyond essentialist thinking and the traditional binary oppositions by which the human has historically been defined. Its paragon, the cyborg, is a hybrid rather than pure being, for whom the technological is elemental rather than optional.[19]

The most postmodern interpreter of our cyborg condition is Donna Haraway, whose Cyborg Manifesto explored the ambiguous meanings of displacement of the central figure of Western humanism as a result of developments in human biotechnology.[20] For Haraway, the cyborg is no longer bound by the ontological and moral categories of the past. Haraway is no starry optimist. She emphasises the political and economic context in which the cyborg emerges as a central figure: that

---

19.   Annemarie Jonson and Darren Tofts, 'I, Robot: AI, ALife and Cyborgs'. in *Prefiguring Cyberculture: An Intellectual History*, edited by Darren Tofts, Annemarie Jonson and Alession Cavallaro (Cambridge: MIT Press, 2002).

20.   Donna Haraway, 'A Manifesto for Cyborgs: Science, Technology and Socialist Feminism in the 1980s', *Australian Feminist Studies* 4 (Autumn 1987): 1–42.

of a globalising anti-democratic capitalism. In this context, a paradigmatic cyborg existence is to be found not in the glossy extensions of the techno-utopians but in the exploited conditions of third world factory women. Nonetheless, Haraway maintains a confidence that even under a cyborg condition, there is hope. She would rather be a cyborg than a goddess, referring to the alternative of an anti-technological radical ecology. Hope rests in the subversive possibilities that the alienated condition of cyborgs open up. Yet it is not clear where the emancipatory hope springs from other than from the moral categories of a residual enlightenment humanism. In that sense the postmodern posthumanists are a mirror image of the techno-optimists, whose continuing humanist ethic obscures the deeply dystopian and nihilistic implications of the stances they take.

3.3 Civic humanism

The third view is that of the civic humanists. These include most prominently people such as Francis Fukuyama, Bill McKibben, Leon Kass and Michael Sandel.[21] For these writers, the application of the new human biotechnologies, not just for therapy, but also for the enhancement of human capacities, would mean a deep alienation of human personhood. Kass, Fukuyama and Sandel have all been members of the President's Bioethics Commission, whose recent publication, *Beyond Therapy* was not a typical technical bioethics treatise centred on the needs and rights of the Kantian agent. Instead, it was shaped by a more Aristotelian conception of the person, constituted in and through moral practices that involve dealing with the given limits, frailty and mortality of the human condition. For them, the new biotechnologies need to be restricted and in relation to some areas there should be prohibitions, not simply because of risks and rights, but more deeply because such developments would erode the very conditions of human personhood.

As the chair of the President's Bioethics Commission and a long standing opponent of abortion and other aspects of biomedical research, Leon Kass has been a highly controversial figure. *Beyond Therapy* has been regarded by many as an expression of a reactionary, bio-conservative world-view. However, as Carl Elliot has commented:

---

21.   Bill McKibben, *Enough! Staying Human in an Engineered Age* (Time Books, 2003); Michael Sandel, 'The Case against Perfection', *Atlantic Monthly* online April 2004 http://www.theatlantic.com/issues/2004/04/sandel.htm

The truly striking thing about *Beyond Therapy* is just how radically at odds it is with mainstream American culture, right and left alike. The report is skeptical of America's faith in technology, worried about America's radical individualism, alarmed at the transformation of medicine from a profession into a business, and deeply concerned about the role of the market in driving the demand for new medical technologies. *Beyond Therapy* may not please many bioethicists, but neither will it please the libertarian or the business-conservative wings of the Republican Party. When was the last time you heard a Republican complain, as the council does, that the pharmaceutical industry is expanding diagnostic categories as a way of selling drugs or express concern that it 'can manufacture desire as readily as it can manufacture pills'? As much as it pains me to admit that anything worthwhile could come from a council appointed by the Bush administration, *Beyond Therapy* is a remarkable document: gracefully written, thoroughly researched, ideologically balanced, and philosophically astute. It will be a benchmark for all future work on the topic.[22]

However, despite appealing to a normative concept of human nature, how this nature is grounded ontologically is not spelt out. Like the others, its plausibility relies on the tacit continuing legacy of the soul or the Cartesian modernist self, and does not involve a serious re-thinking of the ontological grounding of the moral ecology within which such personhood emerges.

3.4 Narrative selfhood and moral ontology
A fourth response is one which, like the civic humanists, appeals to a normative conception of human persons which is articulated through material practices, but goes further in addressing more explicitly the ontological or metaphysical grounding of personhood. Charles Taylor,

---

22.   Carl Elliott, '*Beyond Politics: Why Have Bioethicists Focused on the President's Council's Dismissals and Ignored its Remarkable Work?*', Slate medical examiner http://slate.msn.com/Default.aspx?id=2096815Posted March 9, 2004.

whilst not writing directly on issues such as biomedicine, nonetheless has a focal concern with the implications of a modern naturalistic account of human persons (and thus by implication its expression in technological modifications).[23] Taylor argues that a naturalistic account fails to recognise that to be a person is to necessarily, unavoidably, occupy moral space. It is not a matter of choice whether we have a moral framework (such that our selfhood precedes any particular framework), but that our being a self is constituted within some particular moral horizon. Contra the naturalistic view of human agency as being located in a morally meaningless universe, our very being of personhood unavoidably implies a reality that is ultimately morally meaningful. However, in our post-enlightenment world, such meanings are not grasped scientifically, but within the aesthetic and hermeneutical life of subjective agency.

Taylor tantalisingly fails to provide any more specific account of this moral ontology (despite his own Christian commitments). It remains a generic alternative to naturalism. However, it does suggest that the issues at stake are not to be resolved by protecting the ontological distinctiveness of humans through notions of the soul (or its modernist substitutes) within a mechanistic world, but rather that the categories of moral experience integral to human life are ontologically disclosive of the deep moral reality of the wider world in which we live. They suggest that, despite the seeming success of non-teleological models of nature developed so successfully in modern science and elaborated in modern techno-science, there are paradigm limits which human moral experience exposes. Just as Newtonian physics, despite its enormous explanatory power, was eventually confronted by anomalies that led to a conceptual revolution in our understanding of the material universe, not just at the extremes of speed and space, but of nature more generally, so likewise, human moral experience exposes the ontological limits of a mechanistic world view.

4. A post-Cartesian Christian view of the human person

In this section I shall briefly outline a view of the human person which is both faithful to the Bible and which also takes seriously the post-

23.   Charles Taylor, *Sources of the Self: The Making of Modern Identity* (Cambridge: Cambridge University Press, 1991).

Cartesian challenge of the biotechnology revolution.[24] A post-Cartesian biblical view of persons has, I believe, much in common with the fourth view outlined above, particularly in its narrative view of the self grounded, not in some interior subjectivity, but in a wider moral ontology.[25] In particular, this view highlights the need to resist the bifurcation of facts and values that has been so much a part of the modernist approach to questions of morality, religion and belief in God.[26]

As Stanley Hauerwas has argued, a Christian account of human personhood should not be developed 'abstractly', but contextually: from within the context of the narratively shaped practices of Christian community[27] seeking to faithfully worship God and in turn, the context of a post-Christian technological society. Within this larger context, articulating a Christian anthropology also involves a prior task of reflecting on the limits of the Cartesian/Baconian tradition that still subtly influences the way we think about being human, and recovering an understanding of humanness that is more faithful to the biblical narrative.

Gerald McKenny provides a valuable resource for this process of critical reflection on the legacy of the Baconian tradition. In his book,

---

24. See Christoph Schwobel, 'Human Being as Relational Being: Twelve Theses for a Christian Anthropology', in *Persons Divine and Human* edited by Christoph Schwobel and Colin Gunton (Edinburgh: T&T Clark, 1991), 141. Schwobel comments on the basic common element within the diversity of approaches to anthropological thought: 'It consists in the understanding of human being as relational being. Since modern anthropology largely abandoned the view of the distinctiveness of humanity in terms of the possession of a substantial soul, human being has come to be understood from its relational structure. Most of the relationships in which human beings exist have in this way become the basis for attempts at determining what it means to be human'.

25. Cf Michael Welker, 'Is the Autonomous Person of European Modernity a Sustainable Model of Human Personhood?', in *The Human Person in Science and Theology*, edited by N Gregersen *et al* (Edinburgh: T&T Clark, 2000), 95–114.; *Whatever Happened to the Soul?: Scientific and Theological Portraits of Human Nature*, edited by Warren S Brown, Nancey Murphy, and H Newton Malony (Minneapolis: Fortress Press, 1998).

26. See Lesslie Newbigin, *Foolishness to the Greeks* (London: SPCK, 1986).

To Relieve the Human Condition: Bioethics, Technology and the Body,[28] McKenny argues that modernist bioethics obscures—and indeed exacerbates—the deeper problem of a loss of a moral framework within which the care of the body can be understood. Drawing heavily on Taylor's account in *Sources of the Self*, McKenny observes that the current Cartesian/Baconian approach to medicine is shaped by two moral imperatives which intensify the technologising of the body: the relief of suffering, and the expansion of individual choice. Following Taylor, McKenny argues that these imperatives have deep roots in the Augustinian/Protestant tradition, but have long since been thoroughly secularised. Understood increasingly in secular instrumentalist terms, modern medicine and modern biomedical research no longer provide a moral framework within which technological innovation can be adequately judged:

> In modern [moral] discourse, moral convictions about the place of illness and health in a morally worthy life are replaced by moral convictions about the relief of suffering and the expansion of choice, concepts of nature as ordered by a telos or governed by providence are replaced by concepts of nature as a neutral instrument that is brought into the realm of human ends by technology, and the body as object of spiritual and moral practices is replaced by the body as object of practices of technological control (21).

Taylor and McKenny's 'archaeological' approach to the question of the moral frameworks within which medical research is located and practised helps us to see that there is unfinished Christian business needing to be dealt with in the reformulation of an adequate account of human personhood. What they point to is part of a larger story told, *inter alia*, by Colin Gunton about the displacement of God in Western modernity. This was to a significant extent due to the failure in late Christendom to hold to a truly evangelical, Christological and

---

27. See Stanley Hauerwas, *A Community of Character: Toward a Constructive Christian Social Ethics* (Notre Dame: University of Notre Dame Press, 1981).

28. Gerald McKenny, *To Relieve the Human Condition: Bioethics, Technology and the Body* (New York: SUNY Press, 1997).

Trinitarian account of God, and thus to the meaning of creation and human existence within it.[29]

Recovering an account of human personhood within a Christologically focused vision of reality does not start with an abstract attempt to specify those fundamental features of the human person that are supposedly part of our biological and moral character. Rather, it starts with the central narrative of the Christian faith, and in particular the way that the narrative of Jesus' life, death and resurrection and ascension is not simply God's means of salvation. It is also the paradigmatic disclosure of what it means to be human, both in the sense of the formation of moral agency in the context of a mortal and vulnerable existence, and of the telos of life in the glory of the resurrection. Christoph Schwobel summarises this perspective as follows:

> . . . the revelation of God in Christ is the foundation of what it means to be human. This implies . . . that the true humanity of Christ is understood as the paradigm for true knowledge of human being. If Christ as the Second Adam is seen as the paradigm of what it means to be human, this means that the true pattern for understanding human being is not the factual existence of humanity, but the new humanity in Christ in whom humanity is recreated and restored. From the perspective constituted by God's self-disclosure in Christ the true humanity in Christ becomes the basis for understanding the created destiny of humanity as well as the human contradiction of this destiny and its recreation in Christ.[30]

In the New Testament, the claim that the risen Jesus is the paradigm of what it means to be truly human is expressed most clearly in Romans 5 where the contrast is drawn between the first Adam and the second Adam, and in Hebrews 2 where it is Jesus who fulfils the creational calling of man to be a little lower than the angels and to take

---

29.   Colin Gunton, *The One, The Three and the Many: God, Creation and the Culture of Modernity* (Cambridge: Cambridge University Press, 1993).

30.   Schwobel, *op cit.*

his place of glory and honour under God. It is Jesus rather than Adam
who rightly images God and thus represents the meaning and purpose
of human existence. As Colin Gunton puts it: 'To be in the image of
God is to be created through the Son, who is the archetypal bearer of
the image. To be in the image of God therefore means to be conformed
to the image of Christ'.[31] Moreover, Jesus images God not by the
exercise of the 'god-like powers' that inhere in natural human being,
but by taking up the particular calling to be the suffering servant
Messiah, a journey into suffering and death and thus an entry into a
place of resurrection and ascended glory.

The New Testament presents the resurrection of Jesus as an entry
into that liberty to which humanity, and the whole of creation, is
ultimately called (Romans 8:19). We enter, by faith, into this
resurrection freedom through baptism. Indeed, Christian baptism is
understood as an identification with Jesus in his death and resurrection, through which we are able to 'reign with him' and participate
in the true human calling to image God in the world.

Human life, in this present age, is thus to be lived eschatologically:
in patient and faithful expectation and anticipation of resurrection
freedom and glory in the midst of frailty and mortality.[32] It is also to
be lived in community and relationship. We do not image God in
Christ in individualistic autonomy, but through our inclusion in the
body of Christ, participating in those shared practices of a kingdom
community.[33]

As Schwobel notes, this particular Christological account of the
meaning and purpose of humanness does not deny the empirical

---

31. Colin Gunton, 'Trinity, Ontology and Anthropology: Towards a Renewal of the Doctrine of the Imago Dei', in *Persons Divine and Human*, edited by Christoph Schwobel and Colin Gunton (Edinburgh: T&T Clark 1991), 59; see also Douglas John Hall, *Imaging God: Dominion as Stewardship* (Grand Rapids: Eerdmans, 1986).

32. See Oliver O'Donovan, 'Keeping Body and Soul Together' in *On Moral Medicine: Theological Perspectives in Medical Ethics,* edited by Stephen E Lammers and Allen Vehrey (Grand Rapids: Eerdmans, 1998), 223–238. O'Donovan comments: 'The principle of psychosomatic unity, then, has no free-standing authority for Christian faith and the resurrection of mankind to Christian hope' (231).

33. John Yoder, *Body Politics: Five Practices of the Christian Community before the Watching World* (Nashville: Discipleship Resources, 1992).

reality of the human domain in which we live and the various forms of human consciousness, and social organisation which have been the study of various disciplines—and in terms of which we can try to describe 'human nature'. Nevertheless, a Christological anthropology does not take these as the starting point or the essence of humanness. Rather, from within this diverse experience of human existence we are called into a vocation of imaging God, thereby becoming what we are meant to be.

4.1 Christian anthropology and the ethics of biomedical research

What kind of ethical perspective does this approach give us in relation to developments in modern genetics? I shall touch briefly on three aspects: how we engage in the intense moral conflicts that swirl around stem cell research; how we respond to the remarkable Promethean dream that animates much of the research; and what we make of the emerging biomedical technologies as they diffuse through our society.

First, how does this approach help us to engage more productively in the intense moral debates centred on the perceived threat to the sanctity and dignity of human persons that rightly concerns many people? I believe that it enables us to see that a Christian defence of the sanctity of human persons, including the unborn, is best articulated and defended more contextually in terms of the narratively shaped practices of Christian community.[34] Rather than deploying the more abstract notion of a substantial soul or Kantian transcendental subject, we need to make explicit, particularly in our ecclesial practices, the specifically Christian meaning and telos of human persons, that will nourish our sense of the value and dignity of human beings. This can help to reframe the ongoing 'embryo debate' in a number of ways. It can help to clarify the deeper world-view conflicts that make this debate so intractable, and to remind Christian protagonists of the need to sustain an ethos of missionary communication in relation to their opponents. It can also broaden ethical concern to include the wider range of practices which undermine human personhood (including

---

34.   See Oliver O'Donovan's 'existentialist' (or relational) approach to the question of 'what is a person' in 'Again, Who Is a Person?' in *On Moral Medicine: Theological Perspectives in Medical Ethics*, edited by Stephen E Lammers and Allen Vehrey (Grand Rapids: Eerdmans, 1998).

those of disruptive economic globalisation)[35] and also the pervasive commodification of non-human creatures and the created order.

Secondly, a narratively framed account of human personhood enables a deeper critical engagement with the Promethean vision that animates the drive for discovery and innovation in genetics.[36] Whilst it leads us to agree with the criticisms of the bio-utopians expressed by writers like McKibben and Sandel, we do so for rather different reasons. The sense of limits is not to do with 'naturalness', but with the creational/eschatological logic of the gospel narrative. The idea of genetic perfection runs counter to the narrative of imaging God that Jesus represents. The way of Jesus is not one of increasing control over the world, but one of humble dependence upon the giver of all life. It thus accepts the contingency and mortality of human existence as the creaturely context in which to follow God, and not as a barrier to be overcome.

Yet at the same time it recognises in the utopian dreams of overcoming death, the secularised legacy of the Christian hope of resurrection. A Christian moral framework is not about coming to terms with death as a natural part of life, but that the telos of human existence is ultimately to be found in the act of resurrection. Yet the hubristic approach of modernist techno-utopians is profoundly heretical, inasmuch as it imagines that the threshold of mortality can somehow be overcome through technological means. By contrast the gospel speaks of the death and resurrection of Jesus as the means by which, by faith, we may enter into the liberty of the resurrection. It is through the vicarious suffering of Jesus that we can hope to made whole.

The third issue concerns how we should interpret the theological meaning of emerging genetic technologies. I suggest that our eschatological vision of imaging God in Christ draws us into a critical, though ultimately positive, dialectic with the processes of technological development. In ways that remain hidden from us, the heavenly city, founded on the cornerstone of Christ's death and resurrection, does not simply negate the earthly city in which human

35.   John L Allen, Jr, 'Interview with Anglican Bishop NT Wright of Durham', England National Catholic Reporter May 21, 2004 (http://www.nationalcatholicreporter.org/word/wright.htm).

36.   David Noble, *The Religion of Technology: The Divinity of Man and the Spirit of Invention* (Penguin, 1997).

technological ingenuity is such a central part. Instead it counters it, judging its ever present idolatry and pride, yet ultimately redeeming it from futility. Paradoxically, it is always the hidden presence of Jesus that sustains the hope of the world and its endeavours, that is the 'yes' to human creativity and technology.[37] As Colin Gunton comments:

> The chief basis of human science, technology, craft and art is therefore Christological. The teaching that the one through whom the world was made became part of that world, even in its fallenness, affirms the readiness of that world for human possibilities, but also the restoration of the creation to its telos, its end which is something over and above its beginning.[38]

There is thus a continuing tension and ambivalence towards such human creativity. We are always mindful of its ever present demonic tendencies, and yet hopeful that such endeavours will in God's good grace be incorporated into the heavenly city. This tension is enacted in the central practice of the sharing of the bread and the wine, the act of communal thanksgiving which proclaims the death and resurrection of Jesus and reframes the world in eucharistic terms. Ronald Cole-Turner notes:

> Left unclaimed and unblessed, biotechnology is frightening. Biological weapons and bioterrorism aside, it is easy to imagine countless offences against nature and human beings perpetrated by genetic engineering and biotechnology, even by those who claim well or who act with public approval. Therefore, we want to ask if it is possible, by and in prayer, for the church to claim not just bread and wine piecemeal but biotechnology wholesale, to claim it as God's, to subject it to blessing, and thereby to give it a

37. O'Donovan, 'Keeping Body and Soul Together', *op cit* 233: 'Because God has said his final "Yes" to the world, we may understand the mysterious and world-denying absurdity of death as God's penultimate "No", the No which supports the Yes by refusing all forms of uncreation and destruction in the human will'.

38. Colin Gunton, *Christ and Creation* (Exeter and Grand Rapids: Paternoster and Eerdmans 1992), 123.

meaning beyond its own blind power. If we cannot escape technology's intrusion into the sacrament, can we hope and pray for a sacramental intrusion upon technology, that in biotechnology's visible form as human work the hidden substance of God's work might take on concrete reality? Yet to do so is to act with theological boldness, exerting a claim that is not ours but God's, the claim of God to be creator and Lord of all, even to be Lord of biotechnology.[39]

4.2 Christian community and shaping the practice of biomedicine

Finally, I want to briefly note that this theological vision of human personhood should shape our ongoing practical engagement with developments in human biotechnology. There is an urgent challenge for the church (in the sense of a Christian community gathered as the people of God and not simply as an elite of church leaders, theologians and bioethicists) to develop practices of positive and critical discernment towards the range of emerging biotechnology goods and services. These arise in various contexts: the care of the sick, the area of personal consumption (especially with respect to doing what's best for children); in the area of biomedical research practice; and in relation to the contribution of biotechnologies to economic development.

In broad terms the challenge is to resist the pressure towards individually focused commodified consumption, in which emerging technologies provide a means for greater self-assertion or enhancement within a market society of basically competitive relationships and to try to redirect the processes of innovation and research in ways that are more communal and relational, in which there is a shared sense of the common good.[40] As Cole-Turner's statement indicates, a communitarian ethic of biotechnology is grounded in the central eucharistic practice of thanksgiving, sharing and the symbolic and practical anticipation of resurrection freedom.[41] Rather than

---

39. Ronald Cole-Turner, 'Biotechnology: A Pastoral reflection', *Theology Today* 59 (2002): 39–54.

40. Ezekiel Emanuel, *The Ends of Human Life: Medical Ethics in a Liberal Polity* (Cambridge MA: Harvard University Press, 1991).

41. Adam Wolfson, 'Politics in a Brave New World', *The Public Interest*, Winter 2001: 40: 'In our rush to embrace the new eugenics comparable confusions reign. We are unable to raise objections to it because our view of man is already

uncritically endorsing the Cartesian/Baconian project of relieving suffering and extending human choice, Christian communities can both assess and shape the applications of biomedical research within a framework of moral community centred on the eucharistic following of Christ. This means the primary concerns should be about strengthening the bonds of community, not just within an affluent Western context, but extended in solidarity to include all those with whom we share the planet.

---

saturated with technological categories of thought. One of the most commonly made arguments for allowing parents to increase the IQ of their children genetically is that parents already spend hundreds of thousands of dollars on education to accomplish the same goal. Thus why not allow them to reach this result more cheaply and assuredly through genetic enhancement of their children in embryo? // Formulated as such, the question answers itself. Of course parents should have this "right". But embedded in this question is a very modern, strange notion of the purpose of education: to increase IQ. Traditionally education was not thought of in such limited, technocratic terms. To be sure, parents expected their children to learn the basics—reading, writing, math and science. But education was thought to be much more: It was education to become a good citizen and a good man: it was about the inculcation of virtue. It was about shaping human souls, not raising test scores. If we had not lost sight of what education was properly for, if we had not come to think of it as expanding memory banks and enhancing processing speeds, we would not be open to accepting genetic engineering as a legitimate educational tool. So let's not fool ourselves: A sentiment less generous than education of the young drives the ambition to engineer smarter, cleverer beings. It is the desire for an even more complete mastery over nature.'

Interface 7/2 (October 2004)

Why Should Cloning and Stem Cell Research Be of Interest to Theologians?

D Gareth Jones
Dunedin

1.Introduction

The title of this essay should make us ponder. This is a title that would have been unimaginable as little as ten years ago. It is true that a few theologians were discussing human cloning as long ago as the 1960s and 1970s, but these were the exceptions and even they had never contemplated stem cells. The newness of the topic should itself be a cause for reflection. For instance, were theologians derelict in failing to discuss these matters many years ago, and if they had done so would the debate have been more informed now than it actually is?

With these questions in mind, it is interesting to look at the character of the cloning debate prior to the mid-1990s. Theologians like Paul Ramsey, Joseph Fletcher,[1] and Richard McCormick[2] were concerned with eugenic possibilities, human freedom, embodiment, our relationship with nature, and the meaning of parenthood in the 1970s and early 1980s.[3] While the stances of these writers differed markedly from one another, the debates did point to some important issues that are even more relevant today than they were then. However, perhaps inevitably, the background to the debates tended to be one of extremes. According to one perspective, science was about to lead humanity into a new world order and should be welcomed. According to a diametrically opposing perspective, any intrusion of technology into procreation was a threat to human standing before God and should be rejected. However, the very broad

---

1.   Joseph Fletcher, *The Ethics of Genetic Control* (Garden City, New York: Anchor Books, 1974).

2.   Richard A McCormick, *How Brave a New World?* (London: SCM Press, 1981).

3.   D Gareth Jones, *Clones; The Clowns of Technology?* (Carlisle: Paternoster Press, 2001).

context within which the debates were being carried out at the time meant there was no way in which they could get beyond this crude polarisation.

Looking back from our perspective, thirty years on, it is clear that neither extreme position has eventuated. Science is now viewed in far more pessimistic and cautious terms than it was then, while some of the technology that Ramsey argued so firmly against has been with us for over twenty years. One is tempted to conclude, therefore, that those debates have had limited influence on current thinking, including current theological thinking, about the artificial reproductive technologies. However, the conservative tradition encountered in Ramsey in opposing cloning is a predominant force today in both secular and theological circles.

But what about stem cells? One cannot expect them to have been discussed by theologians before their therapeutic and research potential became a subject of interest to scientists (this in itself is, of course, an interesting phenomenon). However, the use of human embryos in research is another matter. After all, they have been available for study in the laboratory since the early 1970s when the initial attempts at developing *in vitro* fertilisation (IVF) procedures were being undertaken. However, with the exception of people like Ramsey and McCormick, it was many years before theologians paid much attention to this area. Inevitably, even their focus of interest was abortion and the foetus, not IVF and the early embryo. Consequently, when embryonic stem cells (ESCs) hit the headlines in 1998, the theological community was ill-prepared for the rapidly escalating debate that was to follow. This is because the abortion debate with its emphasis on the foetus is of little assistance in determining the manner in which early embryos like five-to-seven-day old blastocysts are to be treated.

The point I am making is that responses to abortion (a negative one, say) have determined response to cloning and the use of ESCs. Unfortunately, responses that slide seamlessly from the older foetus to the early embryo, and from abortion to ESCs, in this manner are likely to be misleading. There is a biological gulf of immense dimensions between the two categories, a gulf that demands nuanced and precise theological understanding.

An additional issue is that the environment has shifted from the womb (*in vivo*) to the laboratory (*in vitro*), and the question has to be asked whether this move has theological implications. Up to now, it appears to have been accepted that an embryo is an embryo is an embryo. Consequently, when it is argued that personhood or full human value is acquired at conception (fertilisation), the location of the embryo does not enter the picture; location carries little, if any, theological weight. In other words, an embryo in the laboratory (with no potential for further development) has the same status as an embryo in a woman's uterus or uterine tubes (with considerable potential for further development). But is this assertion as self-evident as usually assumed?

These considerations are important, not only for the integrity of theological contributions, but also if such contributions are to prove useful in clinical contexts. Society at large, biomedical scientists, clinicians, and patients, need assistance in finding their way through the maelstrom of complex bioethical issues that characterise reproductive biology and reproductive medicine.

2. Dominating motifs

It is repeatedly claimed that humans are playing God, with one outcome of this illicit activity being the design of babies. The impression is given that we have entered a new creative realm, in which we have taken upon ourselves roles previously the sole preserve of God. Indeed, so dramatic has this shift been that we are now thought to rival God. On the other hand, there is deep apprehension that our creations may turn out to be soulless beings who are nothing more than the genetic shells of humans. This is because we as humans are over-extending ourselves by moving into forbidding and dangerous territory, demonstrating all too clearly the ancient sins of vanity and pride. The moral is compelling: designing one's offspring is a role that mortals should leave to their creator.[4]

What we encounter in these descriptions is a strange mixture of theological language and images drawn from science fiction. Together they convey powerful negative messages that leave us in no doubt that we have moved into daunting territory. An example from an American pastor will suffice:

4.   *Ibid.*

> We stand today at a crossroads where quite
> literally the future of the human race is at stake. I
> do not mean the *survival* of the human race, but
> something more sinister: the altering of the very
> concept of *what it means to be human*. The issue is
> not whether future generations shall live; the
> issue is what future people—if we call them
> such—shall be like.[5]

Nothing could be clearer. The theological gauntlet has been thrown down, suggesting that the worlds of science and faith are at loggerheads, representing totally opposing realms. But is this true, and where do scientists like myself, who espouse the Christian faith, fit in? Does theology have anything to offer these debates beyond challenging every biotechnological venture in which humans are involved? Is there no place for a constructive theological contribution to this crucial realm?

One further feature of this debate is the manner in which realistic science and futuristic possibilities are confusingly mixed. Consider the following:

> The age-old human fantasies of the mythical
> chimeras of the ancients, supernatural intelligence,
> wiping disease from human inheritance, designing a
> better human being, the fountain of youth, and even
> immortality now have biotechnical credence in the
> theoretical promises of genetics and genetic
> engineering. Not only can humanity's collective
> genetic inheritance be shaped by selecting which
> embryos are allowed to develop via pre-implan-
> tation genetic diagnosis, but genetic engineering, the
> availability of the human embryo for experimen-
> tation, and combining genes from many species

5.   Erwin B Lutzer, 'Biotechnology's Brave New World', The Center for Bioethics and Human Dignity, posted 21 November 2003, http://www.cbhd.org/resources/biotech/lutzer_2003-11-21.htm.

require only sufficient imagination to catalyze the
designing of a new humanity.[6]

The end-result is similar to Lutzer's, but what emerges here is the
smooth (and inevitable?) transition from procedures like pre-
implantation genetic diagnosis to the reshaping of humanity. Use of
such procedures will lead inexorably to a hypothetical future peopled
by modified humans. The message is clear: stop using these
procedures before it is too late. What is interesting is that this is the
stance of Christian protagonists, whose theological imperatives are
driving them towards outlawing current procedures as a means of
protecting humanity.

The framework within which much of the theological debate on
cloning and (embryonic) stem cells is conducted is dominated by
grand negative vistas, with their overtones of threats to what we are as
human beings. These vistas are dominated by the twin fears that, in
general, we are playing God and, in the reproductive realm, we are
designing babies.

3. Playing God

The forbidden nature of this territory is forcibly brought home by
the notion of playing God.[7] We are going where we should not be
going, we are moving into an area that should be left to God alone.
Additionally, we are meddling (playing) with serious matters. We
are entering forbidden territory, and we are doing so *needlessly*. Life
would be much safer if we left well alone, and accepted that we are
limited beings and that certain things should always remain beyond
our reach. In theological terms, it is often seen as our eating of the
tree of good and evil, succumbing to the temptation to be like God,
and refusing to accept God-ordained limitations.

But does labelling some activity as 'playing God' do any more
than reflect hostility towards that activity? It appears not, since by

---

6. Nancy L Jones and John F Kilner, 'Genetics, Biotechnology and the Future', The
   Center for Bioethics and Human Dignity, posted 8 April 2004,
   http://www.cbhd.org/resources/genetics/jones_kilner_2004-04-08.htm.

7. Andrew Dutney, *Playing God: Ethics and Faith* (Melbourne: HarperCollins,
   2001); T Peters, *Playing God? Genetic Determinism and Human Freedom* (New
   York: Routledge, 2003).

itself it fails to present a clear rationale as to the manner in which it transgresses divine boundaries. Many years ago, the theologian Paul Ramsey commented that human beings should not play God before they have learnt to be human beings and when they are human beings they will not want to play God.[8] Salutary as this statement is, it provides no indication as to what human beings should or should not do in any particular area. The most one tends to elicit from such uses of the term is that the present human form is divinely ordained and should not be modified in any manner, leaving in limbo the numerous uses made of vaccines, antibiotics, surgery, preventive medicine, and genetic counselling. Are these illustrations of 'playing God' or are they not? If they are not, what criteria are being used for distinguishing between the two categories?

Christians contend that humans are made in God's image, and hence are to function like God. Humans demonstrate a great deal of God's creativity and inquisitiveness.[9] In the scientific sphere, this enables humans to probe the creation, attempt to understand it and modify it as stewards of God's creation. In the medical realm, this translates into the desire to control diseases that destroy a great deal that is uplifting in God's world. The aim here is to restore people to good health, thereby expanding their horizons and enabling them to live more fulfilled lives as humans made in God's image. While this ideal is not always realised, and while even such an ideal can be abused, it remains a worthy goal.

From a Christian perspective, it is inappropriate to devote massive scientific powers towards the attainment of superficial and frivolous ends. There are always dangers, and to expose people to these for minor gains is dangerous and irresponsible. It is within this context that it is entirely appropriate to criticise the use of biotechnology for insubstantial ends, such as gene manipulation for eye colour or facial features. However, no matter how justified such criticism is, it is criticism of the misuse of procedures rather than condemnation of the procedures themselves. God-like capabilities are to be utilised in ways that will deepen and enrich the lives of human beings, and not downgraded to become little more than playthings of the rich.

8.   Paul Ramsey, *Fabricated Man: The Ethics of Genetic Control* (New Haven: Yale University Press, 1970).

9.   D Gareth Jones, *Manufacturing Humans: The Challenge of the New Reproductive Technologies* (Leicester: Inter-Varsity Pres, 1987).

Capabilities can be denigrated, or can be used to glorify God and enhance the lives of human beings. As long as the aim of therapy is the alleviation of human illness, it has the potential to elevate God's images.

Nevertheless, there are always dangers, and the notion of 'playing God' should remind us that we are only to modify fundamental biological processes with enormous caution and deep humility. There is much we do not know, and there is much over which our control is tenuous and fragile at best. Acting as God's stewards is an exercise in responsibility, demanding intelligence, compassion and spiritual discernment.

But who is playing God? The assumption generally appears to be that it is scientists and clinicians. After all, they are the ones who make possible the new procedures and techniques, and so it is they who must shoulder ultimate responsibility for the sort of new world into which we are moving. And yet this new world only becomes reality when societies and ordinary people approve of it, including patients, infertile couples, and those of us reading these words. It is we who ultimately make the decisions about what technology we will or will not utilise.

This should come as no surprise, since we cannot claim to be made in the image of God, and then walk away from what that means—exercising responsibility, attempting to improve the world for ourselves and others, understanding as much as we can, and controlling what can be controlled.[10] Playing God like this is essential for God-like creatures and may even be described as having Christ-like overtones. However, at the same time it reminds us that there is much that lies beyond our abilities, and that everything we do has built-in limitations. We cannot do, and should not want to do, anything we like.

4. Designer babies

The term 'designer babies' is also usually employed negatively. Babies are designed by God, and we should be grateful for what we receive—the beautiful, the not-so-beautiful, the intelligent, the far-from-intelligent, the healthy, and the disabled. There is no place for

---

10.   D Gareth Jones, *Valuing People: Human Value in a World of Medcial Technology* (Carlisle: Paternoster Press, 1999).

human interference, since babies are a clear manifestation of the work of God and, hence, are to be accepted as a gift from God. Even the slightest hint that humans wish to interfere with these matters demonstrates an unwillingness to abide by limitations God has put in place.

Unfortunately, this whole area is dominated by a set of *misleading images* of what designing a human being might entail. All too readily references are made to 'making babies to order'. And if this is the case, the assumption is that they will subsequently be treated as little more than impersonal products. It is but a short step from here to the dubiously fascinating and repulsive picture of the factory production of babies. This comes to the fore in connection with human reproductive cloning, with its routinely presented pictures of babies being spewed out of machines in endless identical lines. The trouble is that these provocative images, with their oppressive overtones of a manufacturing process, are applied to any genetic intervention in embryos—change one gene, or discard one embryo in favour of another, and the result is a designer baby. These do not warrant use of the term, even though a currently unrealistic procedure like that of widescale multi-gene manipulation of embryos could well do so.

Biological manufacture is a misnomer. We will never produce babies in the same way as we produce cars, washing machines, or computers, even if we set out to do so. These analogies are, therefore, seriously misleading. If design involves precision and predictability, there is no way in which babies and future human individuals will ever be designed by people like us. This in no way justifies all the procedures in the artificial reproductive technologies, but it should make us ultra-careful that we are not misled by the terminology we use.

So often the focus appears to be on choosing genes for fair hair, blue eyes, high intelligence, startling physique, and good looks, or even for avoiding baldness. The ephemeral nature of these longings only serves to demonstrate their superficiality, let alone an ignorance of the scientific precision, clinical complexities and expensive resources that would be required to achieve them. Unfortunately, instead of demythologising such fantasies as empty claims, they are taken seriously and are used to mount tirades against realistic and therapeutically based genetic choice. The latter can then be dismissed on the ground that its goal is that of producing perfect babies, designed to order.

Dismissal of a host of realistic genetic options in this manner relies upon the introduction of two powerful and emotive themes, namely, *perfectibility* and *design*. It is to be expected that these will convey exceedingly negative overtones for those Christians for whom any interference in reproduction is a step too far. Their message is that science is replacing God by assuming redemptive powers. Salvation can now be found in biological manipulation, with the hope of a better life emanating from genetic intervention. In one fell swoop, both Christ and the kingdom of God have been replaced. The tragedy is that these images stem not from realistic science, but from a fertile imagination. They are far removed from both serious science and serious theological analysis.

What is required is a rigorous assessment of the merits of what can and cannot be accomplished by genetic science. We need to ask what can realistically be accomplished to benefit patients. In this way, the focus shifts to the good of patients, with a commitment to improve the quality of their lives, and, if feasible, to replace illness by health. This is a positive hope, but it is also a realistic one. The genetic intervention may not work and hopes may be dashed. But the attempt is to be encouraged as long as our expectations are guided by realistic clinical and scientific goals. There is no hint here of perfection or of ageless existence in a disease-free body. The dominant value is that of humility, demonstrated by caring for those in need, and of utilising powerful technologies in the service of those potentially capable of benefiting from them (Matthew 18: 1–6; 22: 34–40; Mark 9: 33–37; 12: 28–34; Galatians 5: 13–15; Philippians 2: 3–9).

5. Reproductive cloning

The majority of Christians are strongly opposed to the cloning of human beings.[11] If a poll were to be taken of Christians today, the likely result would be overwhelming rejection of anything even

---

11.   For example, Callum Mackellar, *Creation, Co-Creation and the Ethics of Pro-Creative Cloning* (Edinburgh: The Scottish Order of Chritsian Unity, 2000); Denis R Alexander, 'Cloning Humans—Distorting the Image of God?' *Cambridge Papers* 10 (2001): 1–4; N Messer, *The Ethics of Human Cloning* (Cambridge: Grove Books, 2001); John F Kilner, 'Human Cloning', The Center for Bioethics and Human Dignity, posted 15 November 2002, http://www.cbhd.org/resources/cloning/kilner_2002-11-15.htm

remotely connected with any form of cloning: of human embryos as well as of actual living people. The verdict is in: cloning should be prohibited. But what is it that leads most Christians to be so negative about cloning? Are these views informed by the teachings of Jesus, or are they principally a reflection of prevailing attitudes, or are they a mixture of the two?

The arguments that appear to be decisive for so many Christians are that cloning:[12]

- oversteps the limits of human dominion
- violates human dignity
- reduces any (cloned) offspring to a subpersonal status
- requires experiments on human embryos
- makes children as opposed to begetting them
- subverts the uniqueness of human beings
- attempts to exert excessive control over biological processes.

One of the prevailing fears for many is that the cloning of individuals will lead to offspring who have been designed by their progenitors. They will not be allowed to be themselves because they will have been brought into the world to be like someone else, to walk in the footsteps of someone who has already existed. Human clones will have been deliberately designed to suit the purposes of someone else. Consequently, reproductive cloning is frequently viewed as the epitome of all that is wrong with designing people. Almost by definition it imperils human dignity.

However, the extent of the design involved in producing cloned individuals appears to be minimal. Cloning is attempting to replicate someone (imagine it is me) in certain important ways, but it is replicating my weaknesses as well as my strengths, and my ill health as well as my good health (inasmuch as these are genetically based). There is no attempt to improve upon what I have been; it is simply attempting to repeat me (Gareth Jones) in another generation (gareth jones). Even this replication will prove inadequate, because cloning takes no account of environmental influences. Instead of being 'gareth

---

12.   Jones, *Clones; The Clowns of Technology, op cit*; D Gareth Jones, 'Human Cloning: A Watershed for Science and Ethics?', in *Science and Christian Belief* 14 (2002): 159–180.

jones', I would be 'gareth jones mark 2', which may be a vastly different model from the original Gareth Jones. Nevertheless, one of the major arguments against the cloning of human individuals emanates from the design motif. With this in mind, what are the design-related concerns?

The first is the concern that cloned individuals will be *instrumentalised*, in that they will be treated as objects and not as people, things to be exchanged, bought and sold in the marketplace. This is the way in which we treat inanimate objects that have been designed with the express purpose of being sold. However, children can currently be instrumentalised, in the absence of even the merest hint of biological design. Parents make children the instruments of their own ambitions, when they ensure that they follow in their footsteps in the professions they enter, the beliefs they espouse, the political persuasions they adopt, and the sports they follow.

Regardless of whether children are conceived naturally or artificially, they should be accepted for what they are and loved for what they are. Existence must be in the best interests of the child who must then be given the freedom to develop as a unique individual. Unfortunately, some clones probably would be treated in an instrumental fashion, but by the same token others probably would not. In other words, the way in which people are treated depends upon a host of factors, only one of which may be the manner in which they were conceived.

A second concern, which may be more directly applicable to the question of design, is the possibility, or even inevitability, that a clone would be forced to *walk in the footsteps of another*. The argument here is that excessive demands would be placed on clones by parents or genotype donors to ensure that they live up to a set of preconceived expectations—to be exactly like mother or father or even a local notoriety. These are legitimate concerns, and yet they rely in large part on why the cloning was undertaken in the first place. They would be relevant if the cloning was carried out for egotistical reasons, but probably not if the motives were to overcome infertility.

To force a clone to walk in another's footsteps would primarily be accomplished behaviourally rather than biologically. Placing excessive demands on individuals or groups to perform to certain expectations in, say, sporting, artistic or church circles, is no more justifiable in these circles (where fertilisation has no artificial constituent) than it would be in cloning. There is no question that it would be tyrannical of a progenitor to try to determine another's fate in this way. However, in a healthy family and social environment, this would be unlikely.

A third concern is that clones' *lack of genetic uniqueness* would deprive them of their uniqueness as individuals.[13] The assumption underlying this is that our freedom resides in the genetic lottery and in genetic uncertainty, and in the unpredictability of our genetic combinations. To do away with such unpredictability is akin to imposing upon clones the predictability of a designed unit.

Implicit within this concern is the fundamental assumption that our uniqueness as individuals stems entirely from our genetic uniqueness. However, identical twins demonstrate unequivocally that whatever the relationship is between human and genetic uniqueness, it is not a direct one. Similarly, clones with identical genetic make-up would be different individuals. One way of expressing this is to say that individuals with identical genetic constitutions will always have different brains. This is because the organisation of the brain is as much dependent upon soft wiring (influenced by the environment) as upon hard wiring (built-in genetically). Environmental influences are not mere after-thoughts or unimportant peripheral add-ons, but are essential for the final form of our brains. In other words, our identity is shaped by the history of our relations with others, and by our biographies, and not just by our genetic make-up, important as the latter is.[14]

From this it follows that a lack of genetic uniqueness by itself is not a threat to anyone's freedom. If an individual's freedom is under threat, additional factors always come in to play. In particular, the individual, especially during childhood, would have been forced to conform to the whims of other people: doing what they wanted, reading what they wanted, responding as they wanted. Manipulation of a developing individual is easily attained using behavioural pressures.

In the absence of such behavioural pressures, clones would have their own sense of self, their own thought processes, and their own ethical responsibility. They would be as uniquely themselves as anyone else, and this would include their uniqueness as spiritual beings. Personhood and identity are God's gracious gift, and not

---

13.   A Kahn, 'Clone Mammals . . . Clone Man?' *Nature* 386 (1997): 119.

14.   D Gareth Jones, 'The Emergence of Persons', in *From Cells to Soul—and Beyond*, edited by Malcolm Jeeves (Grand Rapids: Eerdmans, 2004), 11–33.

something that humans can manufacture or copy.[15] The value of human beings rests upon a dual dignity: that bestowed by God and that which blossoms as relationships are established within the human community. It has little to do with genetic status or manner of fertilisation.

Anyone hoping that the production of a human clone would replicate or replace a previously existing person would be sadly let down. This is another way of stating that the design element in reproductive cloning is rudimentary in the extreme. Any fears one may have regarding human reproductive cloning should not be grounded in the power of designing babies or adults.

These are not arguments in favour of reproductive cloning. But they are reminders that theological arguments should be based on theological reasoning and not on emotive fears. This is what I as a scientist look for in serious theological reflection.

6. Therapeutic and research cloning

I have discussed reproductive cloning at some length simply because that is where so much attention is directed. However, I do not think it is an especially important ethical or even theological issue. Far more significant is therapeutic or research cloning, the cloning of tissues and cell lines, whether looked at scientifically, clinically, ethically or theologically.[16] The usual reason given for this is the therapeutic potential of cloned tissues and cell lines. Legitimate as this is, it is not my focus in this essay. I take this potential for granted, even if in my estimation many of the claims made for it are grandiose and overstated.

Within a theological context one issue emerges as dominant: the moral status of the embryo. A frequently expressed underlying assumption is that the embryo occupies a distinct position quite unlike that of any other tissue, since it is the only source of new life and, therefore, of the next generation. Concepts of the embryo's inviolabilty emerge from this; a new individual is in the making and this new

---

15. T Peters, 'Cloning Shock: A Theological Reaction', in *Human Cloning: Religious Responses*, edited by R Cole-Turner (Louisville: Westminister John Knox Press, 1997), 12–24.

16. Jones, *Clones; The Clowns of Technology, op cit.*

individual is a person with dignity, value, and a special status in God's eyes.

This position has far-reaching scientific implications, since if the human embryo is viewed as having status and value equivalent to that of postnatal humans, there is no room for any scientific exploration of the human embryo. Cloning, in particular, is problematic on the grounds that an embryo is brought into being for a short time (up to five to seven days gestation) in order to serve as a source of tissues and cell lines. Using more dramatic phraseology, a human being is created with the explicit intention of destroying it in order to enhance the life of another individual or group of individuals. Since we would not do this with children or adults we should not do it with five-to-seven-day-old embryos (blastocysts).

This particular theological stance raises a serious consideration, and this is the (biological) nature of the early embryo. Until recently, most definitions of the embryo commenced with fertilisation, setting it apart from all other groups of cells in the body. Now, however, it is clear that an embryo can be formed by a means other than fertilisation. This is what somatic cell nuclear transfer (SCNT) is all about. Cells that have differentiated and become specialised cells in well-defined tissues can undergo dedifferentiation, and can subsequently be redirected to form other cell types. In other words, development can be reversed, thereby casting doubt on the enduring significance of embryonic stages, let alone on fertilisation.

The scientific emphasis has to move from fertilization to the embryo itself. If this is the case scientifically, is it also the case theologically? Now that it is possible to produce an embryo without fertilisation, there is no escape from asking when during embryonic development do special characteristics emerge? Biologists are used to asking this sort of question, but it poses a problem for those theologians who are wedded to fertilisation (conception) as the only starting point to personal life. The challenge posed by non-fertilised embryos will not vanish by reiterating the importance of fertilisation.

Even more fundamental is the latent possibility that any cell of the body may, following manipulation, give rise to a new individual. This amounts to a breaking down of the distinction between embryonic and other cells (somatic or body cells). The manner in which embryos can be formed will diversify, once again directing attention onto the embryos themselves and away from their origin. For instance, how will we value blastocysts brought into existence by the dedif-ferentiation of somatic cells, with the express purpose of producing specialised cell lines for transplantation back into the individual supplying the somatic cells? And what if the blastocyst stage can be eliminated altogether?

At best the embryo will have become an ambiguous entity, and it is even possible that cell lines and tissues may be produced by by-passing a discernible embryo altogether. Arguments based on the centrality of fertilisation will become increasingly irrelevant. These directions raise fascinating theological issues, since they remove the boundary fence provided by fertilisation, and direct attention onto the developing unit itself. Does such a modified embryo have any special status, and if so, on what grounds?

The spotlight up to now has predominantly been on just one side of the equation, that of the embryo. Little attention has been paid to the other side, that of the scientists, clinicians and ordinary people who wish to carry out such manipulations. What are the reasons for acting in these ways, and how may they be assessed theologically?

With this complementary side we are introduced to the balancing perspective that theology can bring to bear on issues such as therapeutic and research cloning. It can scrutinise the intentions of all involved, whether directly or indirectly, in these scientific ventures. Are they directed towards the welfare of human beings and alleviating their needs? Are the expected beneficial outcomes consonant with the scale of the ventures? Is the framework within which the ventures are conducted and assessed one of bravado and arrogance, or of humility and an awareness of their inevitable limitations? In practice, there will undoubtedly be a mixture of motives and goals, but theological reflection should serve a crucial role in assessing this mixture, and determining the nature and extent of embryo interventions and cloning.

7. Embryonic stem cells

7.1 What are embryonic stem cells?
Human ESCs burst into the limelight in 1998, when they were first successfully derived. The attention they have subsequently received, on account of their potential to alleviate a range of debilitating illnesses and give rise to a new genre of medical therapies, has been

88   *D Gareth Jones*

bewildering.[17] These positive vistas have been counterbalanced by a welter of concerns, ranging from the ever-present ethical dilemmas precipitated by the moral status of the human embryo, to a confusing array of conflicting claims regarding the scientific superiority of adult stem cell sources. What comes to the fore here is the balance between beneficence and maleficence, beneficence towards those with serious illnesses (who could possibly benefit from stem cell therapies) and maleficence towards embryos (which would be destroyed in the act of extracting stem cells from them). Unfortunately, the place of beneficence is raised only occasionally in theological discussions of ESCs (an exception is Peters[18]).

It is now well recognised that stem cells are unspecialised cells, which have the ability to renew themselves indefinitely, and under appropriate conditions can give rise to a variety of mature cell types in the human body. They have multiple sources, ranging from embryos to umbilical cord blood, foetal tissues, and a variety of adult tissues. For the sake of simplicity, stem cells from all sources other than embryos are termed adult stem cells (as opposed to ESCs).

ESCs are derived from the inner cell mass (ICM) of early embryos at the blastocyst stage, which occurs at about five to seven days after fertilisation. At this point in time the blastocyst has differentiated into just two cell types, ICM cells and the surrounding trophectoderm cells (which will later form the placenta). The ICM cells are frequently considered to be totipotent, in that they have the capacity to give rise to a complete individual. However, this is only the case if the blastocyst, with its trophectoderm cells, is maintained in an intact state, and if it is eventually placed in a woman's uterus. Isolated ICM cells in the laboratory will not form a new individual. This means that ESCs are pluripotent, with an ability to create all the cell lines of the foetus but not the foetus itself.

What emerges from these considerations is that, within a laboratory environment, blastocysts are 'potentially totipotent' rather than 'actually totipotent'.[19] In this, they stand in stark contrast to their

17. Cindy R Towns, and D Gareth Jones, 'Stem cells, embryos, and the environment: a context for both science and ethics', *Journal of Medical Ethics* 30 (2004): 410–413.
18. Peters, *Playing God? Genetic Determinism and Human Freedom, op cit.*
19. Towns, 'Stem Cells, Embryos, and the Environment: A Context for Both Science and Ethics', *op cit.*

counterparts within a woman's body. Since the location of blastocysts is crucial scientifically, one has to ask whether this has ethical (and perhaps theological) connotations. Traditional ethical debate has taken no account of environmental considerations, its focus having been entirely on blastocysts (embryos) as discrete autonomous entities, as though their potential to become future individuals can be realised regardless of environmental considerations.

A fundamental consideration is that, in order to obtain ESCs, the blastocyst has to be destroyed, since the ICM is disrupted. There is no way of obtaining ESCs and maintaining the blastocyst as a viable entity. Does this matter? Is the destruction of blastocysts at five to seven days after their formation unethical or even immoral? We are back at the moral status of the blastocyst. Or are we?

Did fertilisation take place? At present, the answer will be 'yes', but in the future this may not always be the case. Theoretically, the blastocyst stage could be eliminated altogether. But that is not where we are at currently. The question for now concerns the reasons why the blastocysts were created. This may have been specifically for research or therapeutic purposes, or they may be surplus to the requirements of couples in IVF programs. In the former case, they were brought into existence in order to serve as research or therapeutic tools; their creation and destruction as a source of ES cells are intimately linked. In the latter case, they were created in an attempt to bring a new human being into existence; they are no longer required for this end and hence will be discarded; their creation and destruction as a source of ESCs are not linked.

In neither case is there an opportunity for these blastocysts to give rise to new individuals; their future life-giving role is non-existent. There is no intention that they should do so, while their laboratory environment ensures they will not do so. Although extracting stem cells from blastocysts will destroy them, these particular blastocysts were slated for destruction anyway. Decision-making will revolve around the respective merits of blastocysts that have been deprived of their life-giving ability, and benefits that could accrue to humanity from research and therapy using ESCs. There are ambiguities on both sides of this equation. The production of blastocysts that become available for use in ESC research, plus the research itself, have to be justified ethically, theologically and clinically. Neither is a value-free activity.

7.2 Embryonic and adult stem cells

In contrast, the process of obtaining stem cells from adult tissues is minimally invasive. Hence, there is a major category difference between embryonic and adult stem (AS) cells, especially in ethical debate, where the adult variety is seen as being far less problematic ethically than the embryonic variety. What this highlights is their source, for example, blastocysts (embryos) versus skin cells or mucosa from adults. This is cut-and-dried, and yet the actual identification of stem cells depends to some extent upon the environment. Indeed, there appears to be a dynamic interplay between all types of stem cells and their immediate micro-environment—the stem cell niche.[20] The components of this microenvironment have an impact on stem cells, because they affect the precise directions in which they subsequently develop. In other words, both AS and ES cells demonstrate considerable plasticity.

One conclusion that could be drawn from this is that the plasticity of AS cells renders the use of ESCs unnecessary. However, there are a number of scientific reasons to suggest it would be unwise to draw this conclusion.[21] Even though there are a few confirmed reports of truly pluripotential human AS cells,[22] what is required is far more understanding of the fundamental biological issues raised by this research. Scientifically, therefore, research with both adult and embryonic sources should continue, bearing in mind that AS cells are more problematic scientifically than their embryonic counterparts.

In light of this evaluation, considerable care should be employed in advocating, on allegedly scientific grounds, the advantages of AS cells over ESCs as the source of replacement tissues. In other words, it is short-sighted to attempt to circumvent discussion of the moral status of the blastocyst by concentrating on the scientific potential of AS cells alone.

While the use of AS cells may appear to be preferable to ESCs on ethical and theological grounds, this is only true (and then is

20. FM Watt and BL Hogan, 'Out of Eden: Stem Cells and Their Niches', in *Science* 287 (2000): 1427–1430.
21. Towns, 'Stem Cells, Embryos, and the Environment: A Context for both Science and Ethics', *op cit.*
22. Committee on the Biological and Biomedical Applications of Stem Cell Research, *Stem Cells and the Future of Regenerative Medicine* (Washington DC: National Academy Press, 2002).

debatable) if attention is concentrated exclusively on the embryo. This clear-cut preference is far less convincing as soon as the health needs of postnatal humans are taken into consideration. The therapeutic potential of stem cells, including ESCs, cannot be ignored by any who take seriously the welfare of human beings. This surely should be a theological imperative; to do good wherever this is feasible.

The balance between AS cells and ESCs is never static. It is in a state of flux. This depends in part on the precise state of scientific understanding, which is a crucial backdrop to social and theological deliberations. Another contributor to the flux is theological understanding itself. Fixated as much of this has been on fertilisation and 'the point of conception', it now has to come to grips with embryonic events that are post-fertilisation, or even neo-embryonic events that lack any relationship to fertilization.

The traditional much discussed time-points are fertilisation and its major alternative, fourteen days post-fertilisation—with its primitive streak, end of twinning, and implantation into the wall of the uterus (see, for example, Shannon and Walter[23]). However, each of these has major drawbacks when confronted by five-to-seven-day-old blastocysts. The challenge of this five-to-seven-day stage is its location at a time-point between fertilisation and fourteen days, a challenge that will have to be confronted by scientists, ethicists, lawyers and theologians alike.

7.3 Regulations—issues for theologians
This may seem an unlikely juxtaposition, and yet regulations bring us face-to-face with applied theology.

As one scans the regulations on ESCs worldwide, four dominant positions emerge.[24] These vary from position A, the prohibition of all embryo research, to position D, the creation of human embryos specifically for research—encompassing both fertilisation and SCNT. In addition, there are two intermediate positions. Of these, position B confines the use of ESCs to those currently in existence, in that they were extracted prior to some specified date, thereby prohibiting the extraction of ESCs and the utilization of ESCs derived in the future.

---

23.   TA Shannon and JJ Walter, *The New Genetic Medicine* (Lanham, Maryland: Rowman and Littlefield, 2003).

24.   Cindy R Towns, and D Gareth Jones, 'Stem cells: Public Policy and Ethics', *New Zealand Journal of Bioethics* 5 (2004): 22–28.

Position C allows for the use and ongoing isolation of ESCs from surplus IVF embryos.

Do these positions have any theological correlates? Position A is compatible with the stance that human life commences at fertilisation, allowing nothing to be done to the embryo that is not in its best interests. Such a stance would be expected to disapprove of IVF, on the grounds that its development and further refinement have necessitated research on embryos. Further, IVF programs that incorporate the production of surplus embryos would also be unacceptable since these programs inevitably result in the production of numerous embryos that have to be discarded. By the same token, this position fails to contribute to any research or subsequent therapy dependent upon the use of ESCs. Consequently, its emphasis is entirely on the harm done to embryos, ignoring the good that might accrue to others in the human community through the therapeutic potential of ESCs.

It is in this latter context that position B comes into its own, in that it allows some research on human embryos but at the same time setting out to protect human embryos. This is achieved by allowing research only on stem cell lines already in existence. In other words, the embryos from which these lines were extracted have already been destroyed. Nothing can be done about that, and so it may seem reasonable to utilise those stem cells in scientific research. On the other hand, this position forbids the destruction of any further embryos. In one stroke it gives the impression of placating both sides of an exceedingly contentious argument. Research can continue in a limited way, and some good might emerge from this research. Hence, it is not deaf to the plight of people with severe degenerating conditions who could, possibly, benefit from scientific advances. What is more, those advocating protection of human embryos can feel that their case has been supported, by preventing the destruction of any more embryos for research (and possibly therapeutic) purposes.

How should this compromise position be viewed theologically? Christians who view human life as commencing at fertilisation have reacted in two contrasting ways. One school of thought has berated the position on the ground that it gives away too much. In their eyes it appears to accept embryo destruction, even though it is past destruction. For this school of thought position A is the only theologically acceptable position.[25] In contrast, a second school of thought has welcomed the compromise as a way of taking science seriously while also protecting the interests of embryos.

The striking feature of position B is that, while it is based on the moral unacceptability of embryo destruction, it allows the use of existing cell lines. Since these have been obtained through the destruction of embryos, the policy implicitly accepts the legitimacy of embryo destruction, albeit in the past. If this were not the case, no research of any description utilising human embryos or ESC lines would be tolerated. Position A, with its prohibition of any such research, would be the stance of choice. On the other hand, an unwillingness to move to position C, permitting the extraction and utilisation of ESCs, demonstrates that the destruction of human embryos is deplored. Position B represents an uneasy compromise, made possible only by accepting the use of 'ethically tainted /unethically-derived' material.

However, there may be a problem with consistency of policy. Position B proves problematic in societies that permit IVF programs that produce surplus embryos, most of which will be discarded. Hence, restrictive ESC guidelines do nothing to protect the large numbers of embryos that are being destroyed by IVF procedures. They simply prevent research on embryos destined to be destroyed. It would appear, then, that position B introduces an unnecessary compromise that has neither a substantial ethical nor theological base.

These considerations suggest that, for those whose theological stance emphasises the importance of personhood from fertilisation onwards, position A is the more consistent of the two positions. However, this position suffers from neglect of any interests beyond those of the very early embryo. This fails to do justice to the obligations of servanthood, living in community, loving our neighbours as ourselves, and seeking to bring healing and wholeness to those in need. It has to be questioned whether the whole of our focus should be on the very earliest stages of embryonic development to the exclusion of all other stages.

What about position C? This provides a protective view of the human embryo, within the framework of a more consistent ethical

25.   C Ben Michell, 'The President Should Have Consulted Solomon', The Center for Bioethics and Human Dignity, commentary date 11 August 2001, http://www.cbhd.org/resources/stemcells/mitchell_2001-08-11.htm.

stance. This is because ESC research is limited to surplus embryos from IVF programs, with a procedural separation between the initial decision to discard embryos and the subsequent decision to donate them for research. This allows both the utilisation and extraction of new ESCs, and eliminates arbitrary time limits on extraction.

Can this position be justified theologically, since it accepts the destruction of embryos? As outlined previously, the destruction is of *in vitro* blastocysts that have no future as human individuals. Although produced in IVF programs, in order to give rise to new individuals, these early embryos are no longer required to achieve this. There are some similarities between this situation and that found in normal fertilisation where many embryos are incapable of developing further through abnormalities. In my view position C fulfils a broader range of Christian imperatives, seeking to improve the health status of numerous individuals suffering from common debilitating conditions, as well treating early embryos with the care and respect due to human tissue.

But what about the creation of embryos for research purposes, either by fertilisation or SCNT, and the move to position D? On the surface, this represents a dramatic shift in moral perspective since embryos are being created only for research purposes. I accept this and have reservations about this position. Nevertheless, the differences between positions C and D may be less than sometimes thought.

Position D is important in reminding us that a Christian perspective should ensure that we confront the intentions and motives of researchers, clinicians and patients. What is the rationale for carrying out certain procedures on blastocysts rather than on other cells or tissues? Is there any reason for using human, as opposed to mouse, blastocysts? If we choose human blastocysts, what are the reasons for wishing to use specifically created blastocysts for research as opposed to using surplus ones from IVF programs? In what ways do we think this research will elevate our concept of humans as beings made in the image of God?

Whatever view we emerge with on the respective merits of positions C and D, we should look closely at our character as people before God. Specific answers will depend on a close analysis of ethical and scientific considerations, but only within the context of how we act as people seeking to live as worthy stewards of his, asking repeatedly what might be in the best interests of those for whom we have some responsibility.

Interface 7/2 (October 2004)

A Christian Case for Allowing the Destruction of Embryos in Stem Cell Research

Andrew Dutney
Adelaide

1.Introduction

Stem cell research is not in itself particularly controversial. Everyone is touched in some way by one or more of the health crises that stem cell research hopes to address—spinal injury, Parkinson's, diabetes, heart disease and many more. The promise of new breakthroughs in the treatment of disease and injury using stem cells inclines almost all commentators to support the endeavour. Of course there are several important ethical issues involved that still need to be considered—Is this development driven more by the desire for profit than concern for healthcare? How far should biotechnology industries be allowed to set the research agenda? Is Western culture no longer able to give people a sense of peace in facing the realities of aging and mortality? But it is generally agreed that the potential benefits justify the research effort.

The most intense ethical controversy around stem cell research has focused on one matter—where the stem cells are to be obtained. Children and adults have 'multipotent' stem cells that can be used in research and in experimental treatments. But the most versatile, 'pluripotent' stem cells are to be found in the human embryo at an early stage of its development. Adult stem cells can be helped to differentiate into many different kinds of cells but, theoretically, embryonic stem cells could be helped to differentiate into almost any kind of specialised cell. However, while adult stem cells can be collected without harming the person, embryonic stem cells are collected from the embryo by destroying it.

This is the focus of controversy in stem cell research—do the potential benefits justify destroying human embryos? Christian commentators have presented a range of views.

Roman Catholic teaching affirms that from the moment of fertilisation the embryo's 'rights as a person must be recognised, among which in the first place is the inviolable right of every innocent human being to life'.[1] Some Protestant commentators take the same position. In such a view, the deliberate destruction of an embryo is tantamount to murder[2] or, if some version of the principle of double effect is applied, perhaps manslaughter.[3]

By contrast, in the public discussion prior to and following the introduction of the *Research Involving Human Embryos* (Cth) Bill, in 2002, Anglican Archbishop Peter Carnley argued that the embryo should not be regarded as a human being until after 14 days of development.[4] This is roughly the stage at which it develops the first signs of a primitive nervous system and also about the point at which the embryo would implant in the mother's uterus in natural conception. It also brings to an end the period of time during which an embryo might split to produce identical twin embryos. This perspective has been conventional in public policy at least since the time of the Warnock Report in the United Kingdom (1984), which recommended that the cultivation of human embryos outside a woman's body should be limited to a period of less than fourteen days. Legislation in the United Kingdom and Australia has consistently adopted that restriction. In Carnley's view, then, 'conception' is a process that takes about fourteen days. For him, the destruction of the embryo in research can be justified up until that time.

My own view is like Carnley's, but different in one important respect. In my view it is not so much the developmental stage of the embryo that is crucial, but whether or not it has implanted in the woman's uterus. I hold that the 'conception' of a human being cannot be said to have taken place until (and unless) the woman becomes pregnant. In what follows I will provide a brief explanation of this position.

---

1.   Sacred Congregation for the Doctrine of Faith, *Donum Vitae:* Instruction on respect for human life in its origin and on the dignity of procreation. Replies to certain questions of the day. (London: Catholic Truth Society, 1987).

2.   Norman Ford, *The Prenatal Person: Ethics From Conception to Birth* (Oxford: Blackwell Publishing, 2002), 62–74.

3.   B Waters, *Reproductive Technology: Towards a Theology of Procreative Stewardship* (London: Darton, Longman & Todd, 2001), 124–27.

4.   P Carnley & B Hickey, 'Perth Archbishops Disagree on When Life Begins', *Catholic News*, (2003) http://www.cathnews.com/news/311/26.html.

2 Fertilisation, implantation and conception

In natural conception several days may pass between the time when the woman's egg is fertilised and when it implants in the wall of her uterus and she becomes pregnant. In *in vitro* fertilisation (IVF) the fertilised eggs are allowed to develop for some days before one or two of the healthiest embryos are transferred to the woman's uterus in the hope that one might implant in due course and she become pregnant.

The important point to note here is that there are two distinct stages. First, an egg is fertilised by a sperm (either naturally or by IVF), creating an embryo. Second, the embryo implants in the lining of the mother's uterus, having found its way to her uterus either naturally or by being placed there in an embryo transfer procedure (ET) after IVF. It is to be emphasised that in IVF-ET the clinician does not 'implant' the embryo in the mother's uterus, but 'transfers' it to her uterus from its petri dish. Once transferred to her uterus the embryo either implants or it does not. Whether or not it implants depends on the condition of the woman's uterus and the condition of the embryo (especially, its chromosomal 'normality').

Implantation is a crucial process and one which is largely beyond the control of reproductive technology. It is something that happens in the interaction between the woman's body and the embryo. Clinicians estimate that a majority of embryos do not implant—neither in IVF-ET nor in unassisted conception. Indeed they have no prospect of implanting because of either their own morphology or because of the receptivity of the woman's uterus.

According to recent South Australian statistics, approximately 3.5 ET procedures are required to achieve one pregnancy.[5] That is, since two embryos are generally included in each ET, approximately seven embryos are used to achieve one pregnancy. And this high rate of embryos failing to implant is considered by clinicians to be likely to compare favourably with the rate of failure in unassisted conception. In IVF-ET the embryologist has the opportunity to select the embryos which appear to be the best formed to be transferred; which ought to improve the implantation rate. In addition, the cycle of treatment includes the administration of drugs to optimise the condition of the

5.   SACRT, *South Australian Council on Reproductive Technology Annual Report for 2001* (Adelaide: Department of Human Services of the Government of South Australia, 2001), 45–46.

woman's uterus and close monitoring of her cycle to ensure that the embryo transfer is conducted at the best time to achieve a pregnancy.

So while it is quite true that every human being began life as an embryo, it is not the case that every embryo is the beginning of a human being. Not even most embryos are the beginning of a human being—not in assisted reproductive technology, and certainly not in nature. Whether they are created naturally or through IVF, only a small minority of human embryos are in fact the beginning of human beings. Not until the woman is pregnant can we be confident that an embryo (or at least one of the embryos transferred in an IVF-ET procedure) is becoming a human being. And it is becoming a human being precisely by *implanting* in the mother's uterus. In that process, and not before, a human being is *conceived*.

3. Theological anthropology

To regard conception to have taken place before the woman is pregnant is not just to jump the gun. It is to say that conception takes place without her. It reduces human identity to a set of genes and loses the inherently relational character of procreation and personhood.[6]

The trinitarian character of theological anthropology (the Christian doctrine of the human person) has been strongly emphasised in recent decades. From a trinitarian perspective, God is being-in-relationship. There is no God anterior to the relations between the persons of the Trinity—the Father, the Son and the Holy Spirit. God is the dynamic of relations between the persons of the Trinity.[7] Human being, which is being 'in the image of God', is also a being-in-relationship.[8] And it is my view that, at its most basic, primal level human being is initiated in the physical communion between the mother and the embryo when

6. T Peters, 'Embryonic Persons in the Cloning and Stem Cell Debates', *Theology and Science* 1(2003) 1: 69–71.

7. C Gunton, *The Promise of Trinitiarian Theology* (Edinburgh: T&T Clark, 1991) 148; DJ Hall, *The Cross in Our Context: Jesus and the Suffering of the World* (Minneapolis: Fortress Press, 2003), 239.

8. CM LaCugna, *God for Us: The Trinity and Christian Life* (New York, HarperCollins Publishers, 1991), 288–89; TF Torrance, *The Christian Doctrine of God: One Being Three Persons* (Edinburgh: T&T Clark, 1996), 102–103; PA Fox, *God as Communion: John Zizioulas, Elizabeth Johnson, and the Retrieval of the Symbol of the Triune God* (Collegeville, Minnesota: The Liturgical Press, 2001), 41–52.

the embryo implants in a woman's uterus. That physical communion—giving and sustaining life, full of risk but also full of promise—is fundamental to the apprehension of the image of the Triune God in human being and in each human being.[9]

The same cannot be said of an embryo *in vitro*, formed in the absence of the woman and man who contributed their gametes to the process. From my point of view the embryo *in vitro* is distinguished from the embryo which has implanted in the mother's uterus, theologically and morally, and it may be used in research.

4. Respect for embryos

In my view the embryo *in vitro* is not a human being, but it is still morally significant and should be treated with respect. This respect is based on:

4.1 Concern for the couple for whom the embryo was made

Having been created for the purpose of infertility treatment, it is associated with the longing for a child. Clinicians treat the embryos with the greatest care and respect out of concern for their patients. Researchers need to take that into account in the way they make use of embryos. The informed consent of the couple must be given before any use of their embryos in research is permitted.

4.2 The symbolic value of embryos

A society can symbolise its respect for life in many ways, including the way it accepts limits on the way embryos can be used; for example, by setting a limit on the number of years that frozen embryos may be stored. This does nothing for the embryo as such, but makes for the health of the society.

4.3 Concern for social consensus

A society in which people with passionate disagreements can live together peacefully and cooperatively requires compromise.[10] The *Reproductive Technology Act* (SA) 1988 has been so remarkably long-lasting in part because of its success in accommodating competing ethical positions. But that success has required compromises. Catholic

---

9.   Andrew Dutney, *Playing God: Ethics and Faith* (Melbourne: HarperCollins, 2001), 169–70.

10.   *Ibid*, 50.

people have accepted legislation permitting what they might view as an inherently immoral practice (including IVF and embryo freezing). Clinicans and researchers have accepted limitations on their professional and scientific activities.

To say that embryos may be used in research is not to say that researchers should be allowed to do what they like. The embryo is not a human being, but it still has moral significance.

5. Conclusion

Human embryos should be treated with respect, and limits to their use should be established in law. But within such a legal framework embryos may be destroyed for research purposes if the research is worthwhile and if the people for whom they were made give informed consent to that use.

When it comes to embryonic stem cell research, I tend to agree with those critics who point out that the potential of research using adult stem cells is far greater than has been made clear in recent public debates. I am not convinced that we need embryonic stem cells to advance research in this new field. Nor am I satisfied that we have yet thought through what it might mean for us to pin our hopes for health and wellbeing on an industry based on the destruction of human embryos.

Contributors

Andrew Dutney is a minister of the Uniting Church in Australia and the Principal of Parkin-Wesley College, the Uniting Church's theological college in South Australia. He is Associate Professor in Theology at Flinders University and the Director of the *Centre for Theology, Science and Culture*. Dr Dutney is the chairperson of the South Australian Council on Reproductive Technology, the statutory body which advises the Minister for Human Services on the regulation of clinical practice in South Australian reproductive medicine units.

Graeme Finlay is a Senior Lecturer in the Department of Molecular Medicine and Pathology, University of Auckland, New Zealand. He is a cell biologist with twenty years' involvement in anti-cancer drug development in the Auckland Cancer Society Research Laboratory. He has a BTh degree with a particular interest in theological ethics.

D Gareth Jones is Professor of Anatomy and Structural Biology at the University of Otago, Dunedin, New Zealand. He is a neuroscientist, with an active interest in bioethics. His recent books in the latter area include: *Valuing People: Human Value in a World of Medical Technology* (1999), *Speaking for the Dead: Cadavers in Biology and Medicine* (2000), and *Clones: The Clowns of Technology?* (2001). He is also coauthor of the text *Medical Ethics* (third edition, 2001). He was recently made a Companion of the New Zealand Order of Merit for services to science and education.

Ian Barns is a Senior Lecturer in Science and Technology Policy in the Institute for Sustainability and Technology Policy at Murdoch University, Perth. His interests centre on public attitudes to developments in biotechnology, the cultural meanings of the human genome project, and Christian responses to a changing public culture. He has published extensively in these areas.

Mary Byrne was previously a research officer at Plunkett Centre for Health Ethics in Sydney, and continue to work in health care in New South Wales.

Elizabeth Hepburn IBVM is a member of the Institute of the Blessed Virgin Mary (Loreto Sisters). She has taught at primary, secondary and tertiary levels and is currently the Director Ministry & Ethics for Catholic Health Australia and works in Canberra.

She has qualifications in psychology, education, pharmacology, theology and philosophy (bioethics) and has been a visiting scholar to Georgetown University, Washington DC, and McGill University, Montreal. She is the author of *Of Life and Death: An Australian Guide to Catholic Bioethics*, and has contributed regularly to journals in the fields in which she is qualified. She now writes regularly for Catholic Health Austraia in *Health Matters*.

Next Issue

May 2005

Theology and the Legal System

edited by

Christine Parker

and

Gordon Preece